MW01232426

To

_____

From

_____

X O X

God's Words of Life for Kids
Copyright © 2003 by The Zondervan Corporation
ISBN 0-310-80087-0

All Scripture quotations, unless otherwise noted, are taken from the
*Holy Bible: NIrV Kids' Devotional Bible, New International Reader's
Version*, (North American Edition). Copyright ©1995, 1996, 1998
by International Bible Society. Used by permission of Zondervan.
All rights reserved.

The Devotionals found in this gift book were taken from the
NIrV Kids' Devotional Bible, New International Reader's Version
and written by:
    Joanne E. DeJonge
    Connie W. Neal
    Lori Walburg

Requests for information should be addressed to:
Inspirio, The gift group of Zondervan
Grand Rapids, Michigan 49530
http://www.inspiriogifts.com

Compiler: Molly C. Detweiler
Project Manager and Editor: Janice Jacobson
Design Manager: Amy J. Wenger
Design: Kris Nelson
Illustrator: Sharon VanLoozenoord

Printed in China
03 04 05/HK/ 4 3 2 1

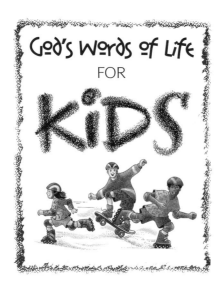

God's Words of Life

FOR

KiDS

FROM THE
NEW INTERNATIONAL READER'S VERSION

inspirio™

The gift group of Zondervan

Table of Contents

God's Words of Life on

Being Different

"I do not look at the things people look at. Man looks at how someone appears on the outside. But I look at what is in the heart," says the LORD.

1 SAMUEL 16:7

O X O

Christ has accepted you. So accept one another in order to bring praise to God.

ROMANS 15:7

O X O

The LORD says, "Do not be afraid
        I will set you free
I will send for you by name.
        You belong to me. ...
You are priceless to me.
        I love you and honor you."

ISAIAH 43:1, 4

O X O

The LORD your God is with you.
        He is mighty enough to save you.
He will take great delight in you.
        The quietness of his love with calm you down
        He will sing with joy because of you.

ZEPHANIAH 3:17

Being Different

Jesus said, "I chose you. I appointed you to go and bear fruit. It is fruit that will last. Then the Father will give you anything you ask for in my name."

JOHN 15:16

OXO

My brothers and sisters, you are believers in our glorious Lord Jesus Christ. So treat everyone the same. ... "Love your neighbor as you love yourself." If you really keep that law, you are doing what is right.

JAMES 2:1, 8

OXO

God treats everyone the same. ... He accepts people from every nation. He accepts all who have respect for him and do what is right.

ACTS 10:34–35

OXO

Think of others as better than yourselves. None of you should look out just for your own good. You should also look out for the good of others. You should think in the same way Christ Jesus does.

PHILIPPIANS 2:3–5

7

Being Different

Suppose people make fun of you because you believe in Christ. Then you are blessed, because God's Spirit rests on you.

1 PETER 4:14

You are all children of God by believing in Christ Jesus. All of you who were baptized into Christ have put on Christ as if he were your clothes. ... Because you belong to Christ Jesus, you are all one.

GALATIANS 3:26–28

God has joined together all the parts of the body. And he has given more honor to the parts that didn't have any. In that way, the parts of the body will not take sides. All of them will take care of each other. If one part suffers, every part suffers with it. If one part is honored, every part shares in its joy. You are the body of Christ. Each one of you is a part of it.

1 CORINTHIANS 12:24–27

Being Different
You Are Just Right

Because you belong to Christ Jesus, you are all one.
GALATIANS 3:28

OXO

All of God's children are one. No one is better than anyone else. What a happy thought!

You are just the right color. You are just the right size. God made you just the way he wanted you to be. God made you just as good as everyone else.

God says that. But life is not always like that. You live in a broken world. God's children are not perfect yet.

Sometimes you may feel like you're not as good as someone else. Someone may think that you are the wrong color. Or too little. Or too tall. But that's wrong. God is right. All his children are equal in his sight.

With God's help, his children will understand. Someday God's children will treat each other as equals. Meanwhile, think this happy thought: God loves his children. Through Jesus they're all equal in his sight.

Try making friends with a Christian who is different than you in some way. Then you can both help each other understand that differences are good and that God loves you both the same!

God's Words of Life on

Being Thankful

We are receiving a kingdom that can't be shaken.
So let us be thankful.

HEBREWS 12:28

O X O

Sing with thanks in your hearts to God. Do everything you say or do in the name of the Lord Jesus.
Always give thanks to God the Father through Christ.

COLOSSIANS 3:16–17

O X O

You received Christ Jesus as Lord. So keep on living
in him. Have your roots in him. Build yourselves up
in him. Grow strong in what you believe, just as you
were taught. Be more thankful than ever before.

COLOSSIANS 2:6–7

O X O

*LORD, I will give thanks to you, because you
answered me.
You have saved me.*

PSALM 118:21

O X O

Give thanks to God! He always leads us in the
winners' parade because we belong to Christ.

2 CORINTHIANS 2:14

God's Words of Life on

Being Thankful

Give thanks as you enter the gates of God's temple.
Give praise as you enter its courtyards.
Give thanks to him and praise his name.
The LORD is good. His faithful love continues forever.
It will last for all time to come.

PSALM 100:4–5

Sing and make music in your heart to the Lord.
Always give thanks to God the Father for everything.
Give thanks to him in the name of our Lord Jesus
Christ.

EPHESIANS 5:19–20

Let us give thanks to God! He wins the battle for us
because of what our Lord Jesus Christ has done.

1 CORINTHIANS 15:57

I will give thanks to the LORD because he does what
is right.
I will sing praise to the LORD Most High.

PSALM 7:17

11

Being Thankful

You gain a lot when you live a godly life. But you must be happy with what you have. We didn't bring anything into the world. We can't take anything out of it.

1 TIMOTHY 6:6-7

OXO

Give thanks to the LORD. Worship him.
Tell the nations what he has done.
Announce how honored he is.
Sing to the LORD. He has done glorious things.
Let it be known all over the world.

ISAIAH 12:4-5

OXO

Be happy with what you have. God has said,
"I will never leave you.
I will never desert you."
So we can say boldly,
"The Lord helps me. I will not be afraid.
What can a mere man do to me?"

HEBREWS 13:5-6

Being Thankful

Sing to the LORD and give thanks to him.
Make music to our God on the harp.
He covers the sky with clouds.
He supplies the earth with rain.
He makes grass grow on the hill.
He provides food for the cattle.
He provides for the young ravens when they
cry out.
He doesn't take pleasure in the strength of horses.
He doesn't take delight in the strong legs of
men.
The LORD takes delight in those who have respect
for him.
They put their hope in his faithful love.

PSALM 147:7–11

OXO

I have learned to be content no matter what happens to me. I know what it's like not to have what I need. I also know what it's like to have more than I need. I have learned the secret of being content no matter what happens. I am content whether I am well fed or hungry. I am content whether I have more than enough or not enough. I can do everything by the power of Christ. He gives me strength.

PHILIPPIANS 4:11–13

13

Being Thankful

Lord God who rules over all, we give thanks to you.
You are the One who is and who was.
We give thanks because you have taken your great
power
and have begun to rule.

REVELATION 11:17

OXO

Give thanks no matter what happens. God wants you
to thank him because you believe in Christ Jesus.

1 THESSALONIANS 5:18

OXO

Come, let us sing with joy to the LORD.
Let us give a loud shout to the Rock who
saves us.
Let us come to him and give him thanks.
Let us praise him with music and song.
The LORD is the great God.
He is the greatest King.

PSALM 95:1–3

Being Thankful
Too Many Things

If we have food and clothing, we will be happy with that.

1 TIMOTHY 6:8

OXO

Some people own lots of things. Often they are trapped by their things. They think too much about them and care too much about them. But they aren't even satisfied with these things. They aren't thankful for what they have; they just want more stuff.

God shows you how to avoid that trap. Forget about things. Think about God. Do not live for things. Live for God. God says not to worry. He will make sure you have what you need. All you really need are food and clothes and a warm place to live.

But God gives you much more than just the basic things. God gives you things that money can't buy. God has promised to care for you. He has promised to walk with you. He has promised to give you peace. Forget about things. Walk with God and tell him thanks everyday for all his blessings. Your life will flow over with happiness!

Church

Jesus said, "Suppose two of you on earth agree about anything you ask for. My Father in heaven will do it for you. Where two or three people meet together in my name, I am there with them."

MATTHEW 18:19–20

O X O

Blessed are those you choose
and bring near to worship you, Lord.
You bring us into the courtyards of your holy temple.
There in your house we are filled with all
kinds of good things.

PSALM 65:4

O X O

You are the body of Christ. Each one of you is a part of it.

1 CORINTHIANS 12:27

O X O

God wanted the rulers and authorities in the heavenly world to come to know his great wisdom. The church would make it known to them. That was God's plan from the beginning. He has worked it out through Christ Jesus our Lord.

EPHESIANS 3:10–11

Church

The family of God is the church of the living God. It is the pillar and foundation of the truth.

1 TIMOTHY 3:15

O X O

Let us not give up meeting together. Some are in the habit of doing this. Instead, let us cheer each other up with words of hope. Let us do it all the more as you see the day coming when Christ will return.

HEBREWS 10:25

O X O

God placed all things under Christ's rule. He appointed him to be ruler over everything for the church. The church is Christ's body. It is filled by Christ. He fills everything in every way.

EPHESIANS 1:22–23

O X O

*I'm asking the L*ORD *for only one thing.*
Here is what I want.
*I want to live in the house of the L*ORD
all the days of my life.
*I want to look at the beauty of the L*ORD.
I want to worship him in his temple.

PSALM 27:4

Church

Because of your great love
I will come into your house, Lord.
With deep respect I will bow down
toward your holy temple.

PSALM 5:7

You are no longer strangers and outsiders. You are citizens together with God's people. You are members of God's family. You are a building that is built on the apostles and prophets. They are the foundation. Christ Jesus himself is the most important stone in the building. The whole building is held together by him. It rises to become a holy temple because it belongs to the Lord.

EPHESIANS 2:19–21

Christ is faithful as a son over God's house. We are his house if we continue to come boldly to God.

HEBREWS 3:6

A single day in your courtyards is better
than a thousand anywhere else, O Lord.
I would rather guard the door of the house of God
than live in the tents of sinful people.

PSALM 84:10

Devotional Thought on

Church

God's House

I was very glad when they said to me,
"Let us go up to the house of the LORD."

PSALM 122:1

O X O

"Come on!" your friend says. "Let's go to my house!" Do you drag your feet? Do you say, "Nah, I don't feel like it." Or do you hop on your bike and head right over?

"Come on!" David's friends said. "Let's go to God's house!" Did David moan and complain? Did he say, "It won't be any fun." No! He grabbed his coat and went!

Do you like to go to church? David did! He was glad when his friends invited him to God's house. To him, going to God's house was like going to see his best friend.

Next Sunday, come along. Let's go to God's house!

God's Words of Life on

Encouragement

Let us cheer each other up with words of hope.

HEBREWS 10:25

O X O

Our Lord Jesus Christ and God our Father loved us. By his grace God gave us comfort that will last forever. The hope he gave us is good. May our Lord Jesus Christ and God our Father comfort your hearts. May they make you strong in every good thing you do and say.

2 THESSALONIANS 2:16–17

O X O

Build one another up every day.

HEBREWS 3:13

O X O

Our God is a God who strengthens you and cheers you up. May he help you agree with each other as you follow Christ Jesus.

ROMANS 15:5

Encouragement

LORD, you hear the longings of those who are hurting.
You cheer them up and give them hope.
You listen to their cries.

PSALM 10:17

OXO

The Scriptures give us strength to go on. They cheer us up and give us hope.

ROMANS 15:4

OXO

My heart trusts in God, and he helps me.
My heart jumps for joy.
I will sing and give thanks to him.

PSALM 28:7

OXO

The LORD is close to those whose
hearts have been broken.
He saves those who spirits have
been crushed.
Anyone who does what is right may
have many troubles.
But the LORD saves him from all of them.

PSALM 34:18–19

God's Words of Life on

Encouragement

God is able to do far more than we could ever ask for or imagine. He does everything by his power that is working in us.

EPHESIANS 3:20

O X O

Let us not become tired of doing good. At the right time we will gather a crop if we don't give up.

GALATIANS 6:9

O X O

Work at everything you do with all your heart. Work as if you were working for the Lord, not for human masters. Work because you know that you will finally receive as a reward what the Lord wants you to have.

COLOSSIANS 3:23–24

O X O

My spirit, why are you so sad?
Why are you so upset deep down inside me?
Put your hope in God.
Once again I will have reason to praise him.
He is my Savior and my God.

PSALM 43:5

Encouragement
Is That Crown for Me?

"I will put beautiful crowns on their heads
in place of ashes.
I will anoint them with oil to give them gladness
instead of sorrow," says the Lord.

ISAIAH 61:3

OXO

Sometimes life hurts. Sometimes people that you love die. Sometimes you lose something important to you. Feeling very sad is called sorrow. Everyone feels very sad sometimes.

People show their sorrow in different ways. In Bible times people put ashes on their heads when they were very sad. But God promised to replace their ashes with a beautiful crown. That meant he would encourage them and help them get over being sad. He promised life would be beautiful again.

Sometime in life you will feel very sad. God knows how it hurts. He promises to help you be happy and encouraged again. He can and he will make life happy again!

Family

How great is the love the Father has given us so freely! Now we can be called children of God. And that's what we really are!

1 JOHN 3:1

O X O

Children, obey your parents as believers in the Lord. Obey them because it's the right thing to do. Scripture says, "Honor your father and mother." That is the first commandment that has a promise. "Then things will go well with you. You will live a long time on the earth."

EPHESIANS 6:1–3

O X O

You received the Holy Spirit, who makes you God's child. By the Spirit's power we call God "*Abba*." *Abba* means Father. The Spirit himself joins with our spirits. Together they give witness that we are God's children. As his children, we will receive all that he has for us.

ROMANS 8:15–17

Family

A father is tender and kind to his children.
In the same way, the LORD is tender and kind
to those who have respect for him.

PSALM 103:13

O X O

Children are a gift from the LORD.
They are a reward from him. ...
Blessed are those who have many children.

PSALM 127:3, 5

O X O

Grandchildren are like a crown to older people.
And children are proud of their parents.

PROVERBS 17:6

O X O

God gives lonely people a family.

PSALM 68:6

Family

Jesus said, "Anyone who does what God wants is my brother or sister or mother."

MARK 3:35

O X O

Be devoted to one another in brotherly love. Honor one another above yourselves.

ROMANS 12:10

O X O

A wise son makes his father glad.

PROVERBS 10:1

O X O

Listen to your father's advice.
Don't turn away from your mother's teaching.
What they teach you will be like a beautiful crown
on your head.
It will be like a chain to decorate your neck.

PROVERBS 1:8–9

Family
Getting Along

How good and pleasant it is when God's people live together in peace!

PSALM 133:1

OXO

Do you always agree with your brothers and sisters? Do you always get along with your parents? No family agrees all the time. You can disagree and still love each other. But if people disagree all the time, something is wrong. If people always disagree, it's no fun!

God says that it is good and pleasant to live together in peace. It feels good to get along with others! God wants you to enjoy your family. Learn to get along. Sometimes let others have things their way. Learn to agree. Your family will be happier. And you will be too!

Think of some ways today that you can get along better with your brothers and sisters and parents. Remember to always try to treat them the way you would like to be treated. That makes for a happy family!

Feeling Angry

Everyone should be quick to listen. But they should be slow to speak. They should be slow to get angry.

JAMES 1:19

O X O

Do not let the sun go down while you are still angry.

EPHESIANS 4:26

O X O

When you are angry, do not sin.
When you are in bed,
Look deep down inside you and be silent. ...
Trust in the Lord.

PSALM 4:4–5

O X O

Lord, you are a God who is tender and kind.
You are gracious.
You are slow to get angry.
You are faithful and full of love.

PSALM 86:15

God's Words of Life on

Feeling Angry

A gentle answer turns anger away.
But mean words stir up anger.

PROVERBS 15:1

O X O

A secret gift calms anger down.
A hidden favor softens great anger.

PROVERBS 21:14

O X O

Don't be a friend with anyone who burns with anger.
Don't go around a person who gets angry
easily.
You might learn his habits.
And then you will be trapped by them.

PROVERBS 22:24–25

O X O

Wise people turn anger away.

PROVERBS 29:8

O X O

A foolish person lets his anger run wild.
But a wise person keeps himself under control.

PROVERBS 29:11

29

Feeling Angry

A man who burns with anger stirs up fights.
But a person who is patient calms things down.

PROVERBS 15:18

OXO

Starting to argue is like making a crack in a dam.
So drop the matter before a fight breaks out.

PROVERBS 17:14

OXO

Avoiding a fight brings honor to a man.
But every foolish person is quick to argue.

PROVERBS 20:3

OXO

Anyone who serves the Lord must not fight. Instead, he must be kind to everyone.

2 TIMOTHY 2:24

Feeling Angry
Don't Do What Anger Tells You to Do

Do what is right. Then you will be accepted.

GENESIS 4:7

O X O

Bad thoughts and wrong actions are sin. It's easier to sin when you are angry. Your anger can bring sin into your heart. But you do not have to obey your anger. You can choose to do right even when you are angry.

If you leave a weed in your garden, it will take over and destroy the good plants. Anger is like a weed. It will grow into sin and destroy the good parts of your life. When anger starts to grow, yank it out. Choose to do right. God will help you win over sin.

What do you do when you get angry? Ask God to show you ways to control your angry feelings and he will help you.

Feeling Sad

LORD, show me your favor. I'm in deep trouble.
  I'm so sad I can hardly see.
  My whole body grows weak with sadness. ...
But I trust in you, LORD.
  I say, "You are my God."
My whole life is in your hands.

PSALM 31:9, 14–15

O X O

My sadness has worn me out.
  Give me strength as you have promised, Lord.

PSALM 119:28

O X O

God, you see trouble and sadness.
  You take note of it. You do something about it.

PSALM 10:14

O X O

Those the LORD has saved will return to their land. ...
  Joy that lasts forever will be
  like beautiful crowns on their heads.
They will be filled with gladness and joy.
  Sorrow and sighing will be gone.

ISAIAH 35:10

God's Words of Life on

Feeling Sad

*I will be glad and full of joy because
You love me, Lord.
You saw that I was hurting. ...
You have put me in a wide and safe place.*

PSALM 31:7–8

O X O

*Lord, you hear the longings of those who are hurting.
You cheer them up and give them hope.
You listen to their cries.*

PSALM 10:17

O X O

*I will be your light forever.
My glory will shine on you.
I am the LORD your God.
Your sun will never set again.
Your moon will never lose its light.
I will be your light forever.
Your days of sorrow will come to an end.*

ISAIAH 60:19–20

Feeling Sad

God doesn't forget the cries of those who are hurting.

PSALM 9:12

O X O

God has not forgotten the one who is hurting.
He has not turned away from his suffering.
He has not turned his face away from him.
He has listened to his cry for help.

PSALM 22:24

O X O

My spirit, why are you so sad?
Why are you so upset deep down inside me?
Put your hope in God.
Once again I will have reason to praise him.
He is my Savior and my God.

PSALM 42:5

O X O

LORD, you have dried the tears from my eyes.
You have kept me from tripping and falling.
So now I can enjoy life here with you.

PSALM 116:8–9

Feeling Sad
No More Tears

God will wipe away every tear from their eyes. There will be no more death or sadness. There will be no more crying or pain.

REVELATION 21:4

OXO

Who can promise that you'll have no more tears on this earth? No one! Even God doesn't promise no more tears in this life. Your world is broken. People get hurt. Things happen that make you cry.

Some shampoos promise "No More Tears." But they don't mean that you'll never cry. They mean that their shampoo may not sting your eyes.

But God has wonderful news! God is going to bring you to his kingdom one day. Then there really will be no more tears! God will fix everything that is broken. And then you will live happily ever after together with God! Won't that be wonderful? How does it make you feel to know that one day God will wipe away all your tears?

35

Forgiveness from God

God is faithful and fair. If we admit that we have sinned, he will forgive us our sins. He will forgive every wrong thing we have done. He will make us pure.

1 JOHN 1:9

O X O

"Come. Let us talk some more about this matter,"
      says the LORD.
"Even though your sins are bright red,
      they will be as white as snow.
But you have to be willing to change and obey me."

ISAIAH 1:18–19

O X O

LORD, who is a God like you?
      You forgive sin.
You forgive your people
      When they do what is wrong.
You don't stay angry forever.
      Instead, you take delight in showing
      your faithful love to them.
Once again you will show loving concern for us.
      You will completely wipe out
      the evil things we've done.
You will throw all of our sins
      into the bottom of the sea.

MICAH 7:18–19

God's Words of Life on

Forgiveness from God

I will praise the LORD.
I won't forget anything he does for me.
He forgives all my sins.
He heals all my sicknesses. ...
His faithful and tender love makes me feel
like a king.
He satisfies me with the good things I long for.
Then I feel young and strong again, just like
an eagle.

PSALM 103:2–5

We have been set free because of what Christ
has done. Through his blood our sins have been
forgiven. We have been set free because God's
grace is so rich.

EPHESIANS 1:7

LORD, *suppose you kept a record of sins.*
Lord, who then wouldn't be found guilty?
But you forgive.
So people have respect for you.
With all my heart I wait for the LORD *to help me.*
I put my hope in his word.

PSALM 130:3–5

37

God's Words of Life on

Forgiveness from God

"I am the one who wipes out your lawless acts.
I do it because of who I am.
I will not remember your sins anymore,"
says the Lord.

ISAIAH 43:25

Blessed is the one whose lawless acts are forgiven.
His sins have been taken away.
Blessed is the man whose sin the LORD never
counts against him. ...
When I kept silent about my sin,
My body became weak. ...
Then I admitted my sin to you.
I didn't cover up the wrong I had done.
I said, "I will admit my lawless acts to the LORD."
And you forgave the guilt of my sin.

PSALM 32:1–3, 5

You forgave the evil things your people did, Lord.
You took away all their sins. ...
God our Savior, make us new again.

PSALM 85:2, 4

Forgiveness from God
Don't Wait!

The LORD is slow to get angry.

NAHUM 1:3

O X O

God is patient. He doesn't zap you the minute you sin. He doesn't push you away because you have done one thing wrong. God loves you so much. He's willing to wait and wait for you to ask for forgiveness.

Jesus took the punishment for your sins when he died on the cross. All you have to do is admit that you've done wrong. God is waiting and willing to forgive you. He gives you time to come to him.

Do you feel bad about something you did that you know was wrong? Do you feel guilty about something that you know was a sin? Don't wait to ask God to forgive you. Ask him right away. He's waiting for you!

Forgiving Others

Love erases all sins by forgiving them.

PROVERBS 10:12

OXO

If your brother sins, tell him he is wrong. Then if he turns away from his sins, forgive him. Suppose he sins against you seven times in one day. And suppose he comes back to you each time and says, "I'm sorry." Forgive him.

LUKE 17:3–4

OXO

Forgive people when they sin against you. If you do, your Father who is in heaven will also forgive you.

MATTHEW 6:14

OXO

Be kind and tender to one another. Forgive each other, just as God forgave you because of what Christ has done.

EPHESIANS 4:32

OXO

Those who erase a sin by forgiving it show love.

PROVERBS 17:9

Forgiving Others
Fight Back with Forgiveness

Jesus said, "Father, forgive them. They don't know what they are doing."

LUKE 23:24

OXO

Your best friend talks about you behind your back. You get angry and say bad things about her. Pretty soon you're fighting. You hate each other. And you're not friends anymore.

Sometimes people hurt you. You want to fight back. You want to get even. But that's not the best way. Fighting leads to more fighting. Hate leads to more hate. It's a nasty circle.

People hurt Jesus. They whipped him and spit on him. Finally, they killed him. But he never fought back. He forgave them.

Forgiveness takes time. First you have to feel hurt. And you have to pray to God to help you forgive.

But forgiveness heals friendships. Forgiving your friend is better than getting even.

God's Words of Life on

Friends

A friend loves at all times.
He is there to help when trouble comes.

PROVERBS 17:17

O X O

There is a friend who sticks closer than a brother.

PROVERBS 18:24

O X O

Perfume and incense bring joy to your heart.
And a friend is sweeter when he gives you
honest advice.

PROVERBS 27:9

O X O

A man's friends should love him
when his hope is gone.
They should be faithful to him.

JOB 6:14

O X O

Jesus said, "I do not call you servants anymore.
Servants do not know their master's business.
Instead, I have called you friends. I have told you
everything I learned from my Father."

JOHN 15:15

Friends

Two people are better than one.
They can help each other in everything
they do.
Suppose someone falls down.
Then his friend can help him up.
But suppose the man who falls down
doesn't have anyone to help him up.
Then feel sorry for him!
Or suppose two people lie down together.
Then they'll keep warm.
But how can one person keep warm alone?
One person could be overpowered.
But two people can stand up for themselves.
And a rope made out of three cords isn't
easily broken.

ECCLESIASTES 4:9–12

O X O

No one has greater love then the one who gives his life for his friends.

JOHN 15:13

God's Words of Life on

Friends

Jesus said, "I will ask the Father. And he will give you another Friend to help you and be with you forever. The Friend is the Spirit of Truth."

JOHN 14:16–17

Let us make a special point of doing good to those who belong to the family of believers.

GALATIANS 6:10

Dear friends, let us love one another, because love comes from God.

1 JOHN 4:7

Anyone who walks with wise people grows wise.

PROVERBS 13:20

Carry each other's heavy loads. If you do, you will give the law of Christ its full meaning.

GALATIANS 6:2

Friends

Best Friends

In the name of the LORD we have taken an oath.
We've promised to be friends.

1 SAMUEL 20:42

OXO

Friends bring joy to your life. They're special gifts from God.

David and Jonathan were friends in the Bible that really valued their friendship. They promised to be friends forever. Jonathan saved David's life more than once. And, years later, King David remembered his friend. He found Jonathan's son and treated him royally. What a beautiful friendship!

Friends love each other. Friends help each other. Friends cry with each other. Friends laugh with each other.

Good friends can remind you of God. You understand a bit of God's love through them. You feel a bit of God's help through them. You enjoy a bit of God's comfort through them.

The friends you have now could be forever friends. Have fun with them. Love them. Tell your friends how much they mean to you. And thank God for them!

Giving to Others

I once was young, and now I'm old.
But I've never seen godly people deserted.
I've never seen their children begging
for bread.
The godly are always giving and lending freely.
Their children will be blessed.

PSALM 37:25–26

Your gifts meet the needs of God's people. And that's not all. Your gifts also cause many people to thank God.

2 CORINTHIANS 9:12

O X O

Give freely to those who are needy. Open your hearts to them. Then the LORD your God will bless you in all your work. He will bless you in everything you do.

DEUTERONOMY 15:10

O X O

Good things will come to those who are willing to
lend freely.
Good things will come to those who are fair
in everything they do.
They will always be secure.
Those who do what is right will be
remembered forever.

　　　PSALM 112:5–6

Giving to Others

God supplies seed to the planter. He supplies bread for food. God will also supply and increase the amount of your seed. He will increase the results of your good works. You will be made rich in every way. Then you can always give freely.

2 CORINTHIANS 9:10–11

O X O

Anyone who gives a lot will succeed.
Anyone who renews others will be renewed.

PROVERBS 11:25

O X O

Anyone who gives freely will be blessed.
That's because he shares his food with
those who are poor.

PROVERBS 22:9

O X O

Give, and it will be given to you. A good amount will be poured into your lap. It will be pressed down, shaken together, and running over. The same amount you give will be measured out to you.

LUKE 6:38

God's Words of Life on

Giving to Others

You should each give what you have decided in your heart to give. You shouldn't give if you don't want to. You shouldn't give because you are forced to. God loves a cheerful giver. And God is able to shower all kinds of blessings on you. In all things and at all times you will have everything you need. You will do more and more good works. It is written, *"They have spread their gifts around to poor people. Their good works continue forever."*

2 CORINTHIANS 9:6–9

OXO

Those who are godly give freely to others. The LORD will give the land to those he blesses.

PSALM 37:21–22

OXO

Godly people give without holding back.

PROVERBS 21:26

OXO

Those who give to poor people will have everything they need.

PROVERBS 28:27

Giving to Others
Plant Many Seeds

Here is something to remember. The one who plants only a little will gather only a little. And the one who plants a lot will gather a lot.

2 CORINTHIANS 9:6

OXO

Pretend that you will plant a garden. You have many tomato seeds. Will you plant just a few seeds? Of course not! You will use all of your seeds. You will plant them freely. Then many tomato plants will grow.

Now it is time to pick the tomatoes. Thick, healthy tomato plants crowd your garden. Plump, juicy tomatoes are ready to eat. You have more than enough. You have enough for all your friends.

Inside each tomato you can find more seeds. You have lots of seeds to plant next year. Aren't you glad you planted the seeds freely?

God wants you to give freely, too. Don't keep all your blessings to yourself. Share with others.

When you give freely, God will give freely to you. He'll give you more than enough. You can share those blessings too. You'll still have plenty, just like tomato seeds.

Even if you don't have lots of money or things to give away, you can share your time and your love with others. Those are the best things you can give!

God Helps You

When I was in trouble, I called out to the LORD.
I cried to my God for help.
From his temple he heard my voice.
My cry for help reached his ears. ...
He reached down from heaven. He took hold of me.
He lifted me out of the deep waters.

PSALM 18:6, 16

God has not forgotten the one who is hurting.
He has not turned away from his suffering.
He has not turned his face away from him.
He has listened to his cry for help.

PSALM 22:24

The LORD gives me strength. He is like a shield that
keeps me safe.
My heart trusts in him and he helps me.

PSALM 28:7

LORD my God, I called out to you for help.
And you healed me.

PSALM 30:2

God's Words of Life

God Helps You

I was afraid and said,
   "I've been cut off from you!"
But you heard my cry for your favor, Lord.
      You heard me when I called out to you for help.

PSALM 31:22

O X O

We wait in hope for the Lord.
      He helps us. He is like a shield
         that keeps us safe.

PSALM 33:20

O X O

The Lord saves those who do what is right.
      He is their place of safety when trouble comes.
The Lord helps them and saves them.
      He saves them from sinful people
      because they go to him for safety.

PSALM 37:39–40

O X O

God is our place of safety. He gives us strength.
      He is always there to help us in times
         of trouble.

PSALM 46:1

God's Words of Life

God Helps You

I know that God helps me.
>*The Lord is the one who keeps me going.*

PSALM 54:4

O X O

Because you have helped me,
>*I sing in the shadow of your wings.*
I hold on to you.
>*Your powerful right hand takes good care of*
>*me, Lord.*

PSALM 63:7–8

O X O

I look up to the hills.
>*Where does my help come from?*
My help comes from the LORD.
>*He is the Maker of heaven and earth.*

PSALM 121:1–2

O X O

"I will make you strong and help you.
>*My powerful right hand will take*
>>*good care of you.*
>*I always do what is right," says the Lord.*

ISAIAH 41:10

God Helps You

Have No Fear
God is Here!

Here is what I'm commanding you to do. Be strong and brave. Do not be terrified. Do not lose hope. I am the LORD your God. I will be with you every-where you go.

JOSHUA 1:9

O X O

God sent Joshua out to do a big job. He had to lead God's people into the Promised Land. They would have to fight to get their land. It was scary, but they had to have hope.

God told Joshua to be strong and brave! He felt weak, but God made him strong. He felt scared, but God made him brave. Joshua knew he was doing what God told him to do. So he knew God would help him.

When you are doing what God wants, God will help you too. He will give you power. He will help you be strong and brave. So, dare to do what God wants! Be brave! Feel God's power in you!

God Keeps You Safe

I will lie down and sleep in peace.
LORD, you alone keep me safe.

PSALM 4:8

OXO

The Most High God is like a shield that keeps me safe.
He saves those whose hearts are honest.

PSALM 7:10

OXO

LORD, you will keep us safe.
You will always keep sinners from hurting us.

PSALM 12:7

OXO

God keep me safe.
I go to you for safety.
I said to the LORD, "You are my Lord."
Without you, I don't have anything
that is good."

PSALM 16:1–2

God Keeps You Safe

Show the wonder of your great love, Lord.
By using your powerful right hand,
You save those who go to you for safety
from their enemies.
Take good care of me, just as you would take care
of your own eyes.
Hide me in the shadow of your wings.

PSALM 17:7–8

O X O

The LORD is my rock and my fort. He is the One
who saves me.
My God is my rock. I go to him for safety.
He is like shield to me. He's the power that
saves me. He's my place of safety.

PSALM 18:2

O X O

Jesus said, "See that you don't look down on one of these little ones. Here is what I tell you. Their angels in heaven can go at any time to see my Father who is in heaven."

MATTHEW 18:10

God Keeps You Safe

I cry out to God Most High.
I cry out to God, and he carries out his plan
for me.
He answers from heaven and saves me.
He puts to shame those who chase me.
He shows me his love and his truth.

PSALM 57:2–3

Our people of long ago put their trust in you, Lord.
They trusted in you, and you saved them.
They cried out to you and were saved.
They trusted in you, and you didn't let
them down.

PSALM 22:4–5

When I'm in trouble,
God will keep me safe in his house.
He will hide me in the safety of his holy tent.
He will put me on a rock that is very high.

PSALM 27:5

The Lord is faithful. He will strengthen you. He will
guard you from the evil one.

2 THESSALONIANS 3:3

God Keeps You Safe

The LORD saves those who do what is right.
He is their place of safety when trouble comes.
The LORD helps them and saves them.
He saves them from sinful people because
they go to him for safety.

PSALM 37:39–40

O X O

Let all those who go to you for safety be glad, LORD.
Let them always sing with joy.
Spread your cover over them and keep them safe.
Then those who love you will be glad
because of you.
LORD, you bless those who do what is right.
Like a shield, your loving care keeps them safe.

PSALM 5:11–12

O X O

The Lord says, "You will pass through deep waters.
But I will be with you.
You will pass through the rivers.
But their waters will not sweep over you.
You will walk through fire.
But you will not be burned.
The flames will not harm you."

ISAIAH 43:2

57

God Keeps You Safe

The Lord loves those who are honest.
    He will not desert those who are faithful
    to him.
They will be kept safe forever.

PSALM 37:28

OXO

God stores up success for honest people
    He is like a shield to those who live without
        blame. He keeps them safe.
He guards the path of those who are honest.
    He watches over the way of his faithful ones.

PROVERBS 2:7–8

OXO

You are my hiding place, Lord.
    You will keep me safe from trouble.
You will surround me with songs sung by those
        who praise you
    because you save your people.

PSALM 32:7

OXO

The angel of the Lord stands guard
    around those who have respect for him.
    And he saves them.

PSALM 34:7

God Keeps You Safe

The person who rests in the shadow of the Most
        High God
        Will be kept safe by the Mighty One.
I will say about the Lord,
        "He is my place of safety
He is like a fort to me.
        He is my God. I trust in him."
He will certainly save you from hidden traps.
        and from deadly sickness.
He will cover you with his wings.
        Under the feathers of his wings you will
        find safety.
        He is faithful. He will keep you safe like a
        shield or a tower.
You won't have to be afraid of the terrors that
        come during the night.
        You won't have to fear the arrows that come
        at you during the day.
You won't have to be afraid of the sickness that
        attacks in the darkness. ...
The LORD is the one who keeps you safe.
        So let the Most High God be like a
        home to you.
Then no harm will come to you. ...
The LORD will command his angels
        to take good care of you.
They will lift you up in their hands.
        Then you won't trip over a stone.

PSALM 91:1–6, 9–12

God's Words of Life

God Keeps You Safe

May my honest and good life keep me safe.
I have put my hope in you, Lord.

PSALM 25:21

O X O

Save your people, Lord. Bless those who belong
to you.
Be their shepherd. Take care of them forever.

PSALM 28:9

O X O

LORD, you keep the lamp of my life burning brightly.
You are my God. You bring light into my
darkness.

PSALM 18:28

O X O

The LORD will go ahead of you and lead you.
The God of Israel will follow behind you and
guard you.

ISAIAH 52:12

O X O

God guards the lives of those who are faithful to him.
He saves them from the power of sinful
people.

PSALM 97:10

God Keeps You Safe

On Daddy's Shoulders

You also saw how the LORD your God brought you through the desert. He carried you everywhere you went, just as a father carries his son.

DEUTERONOMY 1:31

OXO

Think of a time when someone strong carried you on his shoulders. Remember how safe you felt? God wants you to feel that safe with him. God is strong. When you are in danger, God will protect you. He can help keep you safe.

God doesn't really pick you up and put you on his shoulders. But he is with you to watch over you. You can feel as safe with God as a child feels on Daddy's shoulders. God is stronger than anyone. He is always with you. And he is there to help keep you safe. When you feel weak, remember God is strong.

God's Words of Life

God Made You Special

How you made me is amazing and wonderful, Lord.
  I praise you for that.
What you have done is wonderful.
  I know that very well.
None of my bones was hidden from you
    when you made me inside my mother's body.
    That place was dark as the deepest parts of
      the earth.
When you were putting me together there,
    your eyes saw my body even before it was
      formed.
You planned how many days I would live.
    You wrote down the number of them in
      your book
    before I had lived through even one of them.
God your thoughts about me are priceless.
    No one can possibly add them all up.

PSALM 139:14–17

O X O

"Before I formed you in your mother's body
    I chose you.
    Before you were born I set you apart to
      serve me," says the Lord.

JEREMIAH 1:5

I have made you. And I will carry you.
I will take care of you. And I will save you.
    I am the LORD.

ISAIAH 46:4

God Made You Special

God said, "Let us make man in our likeness. Let them rule over the fish in the waters and the birds of the air. Let them rule over the livestock and over the whole earth. Let them rule over all of the creatures that move along the ground."
So God created man in his own likeness
   He created him in the likeness of God.
   He created them as male and female.
God blessed them.

GENESIS 1:26–28

O X O

Anyone who believes in Christ is a new creation. The old is gone! The new has come!

2 CORINTHIANS 5:17

O X O

God chose us to belong to Christ before the world was created. He chose us to be holy and without blame in his eyes. He loved us.

EPHESIANS 1:4

God Made You Special

God says, "I will send for you by name.
You belong to me."

ISAIAH 43:1

O X O

God made us. He created us to belong to Christ Jesus. Now we can do good things. Long ago God prepared them for us to do.

EPHESIANS 2:10

O X O

God chose us to give us new birth through the message of truth. He wanted us to be the first and best of everything he created.

JAMES 1:18

O X O

The LORD God formed a man. He made him out of the dust of the ground. He breathed the breath of life into him. And the man became a living person.

GENESIS 2:7

O X O

"You are priceless to me.
I love you and honor you," says the Lord.

ISAIAH 43:4

God Made You Special
Amazing and Wonderful

You created the deepest parts of my being, Lord.
You put me together inside my mother's body.

PSALM 139:13

OXO

God gave you an absolutely wonderful body! You have more parts than you can imagine. You have more than 600 muscles. You have thousands of hairs. You have billions of nerves.

Some parts work all by themselves. Put your hand over your heart. Feel it beat. It will beat as long as you live. Your heart works all by itself.

You don't have to remember to breathe. You can forget about that. Your body will breathe all by itself.

Can you imagine everything that happens in your body? Can you know about all its parts? No human can.

Only God fully understands your body. He knows how it works. He made you. And he made you the only you in the world. You're special!

Only God completely understands you. But God also loves you. He watches over you all the time. Aren't you glad?!

God's Words of Life

God Saves You

God loved the world so much that he gave his one and only Son. Anyone who believes in him will not die but will have eternal life.

JOHN 3:16

Even though you have not seen Jesus, you love him. Though you do not see him now, you believe in him. You are filled with a glorious joy that can't be put into words. You are receiving the salvation of your souls. It is the result of your faith.

1 PETER 1:8–9

Christ took away the sins of many people. He will also come a second time. At that time he will not suffer for sin. Instead he will come to bring salvation to those who are waiting for him.

HEBREWS 9:28

Say with your mouth, "Jesus is Lord." Believe in your heart that God raised him from the dead. Then you will be saved.

ROMANS 10:9

God Saves You

Give praise to the God and Father of our Lord Jesus Christ. In his great mercy he has given us a new birth and a hope that is alive. It is alive because Jesus Christ rose from the dead. He has given us new birth so that we might share in what belongs to him. It is a gift that can never be destroyed. It can never spoil or even fade away. It is kept in heaven for you. Through faith you are kept safe by God's power. Your salvation is going to be completed.

1 PETER 1:3–5

God's grace has saved you because of your faith in Christ. Your salvation doesn't come from anything you do. It is God's gift. It is not based on anything you have done.

EPHESIANS 2:8–9

God didn't choose us to receive his anger. He chose us to receive salvation because of what our Lord Jesus Christ has done.

1 THESSALONIANS 5:9

God Saves You

The LORD gives me strength. I sing about him.
He has saved me.

EXODUS 15:2

O X O

God poured out the Spirit on us freely because of what Jesus Christ our Savior has done. His grace made us right with God. So now we have received the hope of eternal life as God's children.

TITUS 3:6–7

O X O

We have put our hope in the living God. He is the Savior of all people. Most of all he is the Savior of those who believe.

1 TIMOTHY 4:10

O X O

God loves us deeply. He is full of mercy. So he gave us new life because of what Christ has done. He gave us life even when we were dead in sin. God's grace has saved you.

EPHESIANS 2:4–5

O X O

Everyone who calls on the name of the Lord will be saved.

ROMANS 10:13

God Saves You

No one has ever seen God. But if we love one another God lives in us. His love is made complete in us.

1 JOHN 4:12

O X O

People now come to God through Jesus. And he is able to save them completely for all time…. He prays for them.

HEBREWS 7:25

O X O

I am not ashamed of the good news. It is God's power. And it will save everyone who believes.

ROMANS 1:16

O X O

Jesus said, "I am the way and the truth and the life. No one comes to the Father except through me."

JOHN 14:6

O X O

Jesus said, "I am the resurrection and the life. Anyone who believes in me will live, even if he dies. And those who live and believe in me will never die."

JOHN 11:25–26

God Saves You

We are made right with God by putting our faith in Jesus Christ. That happens to all who believe. ... Everyone has sinned. No one measures up to God's glory. The free gift of God's grace makes all of us right with him. Christ Jesus paid the price to set us free.

ROMANS 3:22–24

OXO

You also became believers in Christ. That happened when you heard the message of truth. It was the good news about how you could be saved. When you believed, he marked you with a seal. The seal is the Holy Spirit that he promised. The Spirit marks us as God's own. We can now be sure that someday we will receive all that God has promised. That will happen after God sets all of his people completely free. All of those things will bring praise to his glory.

EPHESIANS 1:13–14

OXO

Everyone who is a child of God has won the battle over the world. Our faith has won the battle for us. Who is it that has won the battle over the world? Only the person who believes that Jesus is the Son of God.

1 JOHN 5:4–5

God Saves You
God Makes It Simple

You can't be saved by believing in anyone else.

ACTS 4:12

OXO

How can you be saved from your sins? Some people make it seem so hard. God makes it so simple.

Some people make many rules. "You can't do this." "You must do that." God says just to believe in Jesus.

Some people try to earn their salvation. They think they must live a perfect life. God says that only Jesus is perfect. He lived the perfect life for you.

Some people say that Jesus is not enough. They try to follow other leaders too. God says that you only need Jesus.

Some people pray to nature. But God made everything. Only God should receive your prayers. Only God saves you.

God makes it all so simple. You need only Jesus. He loves you. He died and then rose from the dead to save you. Just believe in Jesus and you will live forever with God one day!

God Shows You What to Do

God guides me in the right paths
for the honor of his name.

PSALM 23:3

O X O

Your word is like a lamp that shows me the way, Lord.
It is like a light that guides me.

PSALM 119:105

O X O

Send out your light and your truth, Lord.
Let them guide me.
Let them bring me back to your holy mountain,
to the place where you live.

PSALM 43:3

O X O

God is our God for ever and ever.
He will be our guide to the very end.

PSALM 48:14

O X O

You are my rock and my fort, O God.
Lead me and guide me for the honor of
your name.

PSALM 31:3

God Shows You What to Do

In the morning let me hear about your faithful love,
because I've put my trust in you, Lord.
Show me the way I should live,
because I pray to you.

PSALM 143:8

O X O

Suppose I were to rise with the sun in the east
and then cross over to the west where it
sinks into the ocean.
Your hand would always be there to guide me, Lord.
Your right hand would still be holding
me close.

PSALM 139:9–10

O X O

When the Spirit of truth comes, he will guide you
into all truth.

JOHN 16:13

O X O

Lord, show me your ways.
Teach me how to follow you.
Guide me in your truth. Teach me.
You are God my Savior.
I put my hope in you all day long.

PSALM 25:4–5

God Shows You What to Do

The LORD is the Holy One of Israel.
He sets his people free. He says to them,
"I am the LORD your God.
I teach you what is best for you.
I direct you in the way you should go."

ISAIAH 48:17

OXO

You give me wise advice to guide me, Lord.

PSALM 73:24

OXO

You always show me the path that leads to life, Lord.
You will fill me with joy when I am with you.
You will give me endless pleasures at your
right hand.

PSALM 16:11

OXO

The LORD says, "Stand where the roads cross, and
look around.
Ask where the old paths are.
Ask for the good path, and walk on it.
Then your hearts will find rest in me."

JEREMIAH 6:16

God Shows You What to Do

Led by a Cloud

The cloud of the LORD was above the holy tent during the day. Fire was in the cloud at night. The whole community of Israel could see the cloud during all of their travels.

EXODUS 40:38

OXO

The Israelites were on their way to Canaan. But they did not have maps or guides. And there were enemies all around. Which way should they go?

God led them. He sent a cloud that everyone could see. When the cloud moved, they moved. When the cloud stayed, they stayed. At night, he filled the cloud with fire. So every day and every night, the Israelites knew where to go.

How do you know where to go and what to do? God does not send a cloud to guide you. But he gave you his Word. He gave you his Spirit. He gave you people who love you. That's better than a cloud any day!

Keep your eyes and your heart open every day for the special ways that God guides you and shows you what you should do. He promises to guide you!

God's Words of Life

God Teaches You

LORD, teach me your ways.
Lead me along a straight path.

PSALM 27:11

O X O

"I will guide you and teach you the way you
should go.
I will give you good advice and watch over
you," says the Lord.

PSALM 32:8

O X O

Listen to your father's advice.
Don't turn away from your mother's teaching.
What they teach you will be like a beautiful crown
on your head.
It will be like a chain to decorate your neck.

PROVERBS 1:8–9

O X O

I know that you want truth to be in my heart.
You teach me wisdom deep down inside
me, Lord.

PSALM 51:6

O X O

Everything that was written in the past was written
to teach us. The Scriptures give us strength to go
on. They cheer us up and give us hope.

ROMANS 15:4

God Teaches You

I give you good advice.
So don't turn away from what I teach you.
I was once a young boy in my father's house.
I was my mother's only child.
My father taught me.
He said, "Hold on to my words with all your
heart.
Keep my commands. Then you will live.
Get wisdom. Get understanding.
Don't forget my words. Don't turn away
from them.
Stay close to wisdom, and she will keep you safe
Love her, and she will watch over you.
Wisdom is best. So get wisdom.
No matter what it costs, get understanding.
Value wisdom, and she will lift you up.
Hold her close, and she will honor you.
She will set a beautiful crown on your head.
She will give you a glorious crown."

PROVERBS 4:2–9

LORD, teach me how you want me to live.
Then I will follow your truth.
Give me a heart that doesn't want anything
more than to worship you.

PSALM 86:11

God Teaches You

Jesus said, "Become my servants and learn from me. I am gentle and free of pride. You will find rest for your souls. Serving me is easy, and my load is light."

MATTHEW 11:29–30

O X O

God shows those who aren't proud how to do
what is right.
He teaches them his ways.

PSALM 25:9

O X O

If any of you need wisdom, ask God for it. He will give it to you. God gives freely to everyone.

JAMES 1:5

O X O

I haven't turned away from your laws, Lord,
because you yourself have taught me.
Your words are very sweet to my taste!
They are sweeter than honey to me.

PSALM 119:102–103

O X O

Your heart will become wise.
Your mind will delight in knowledge.
Good sense will keep you safe.
Understanding will guard you.

PROVERBS 2:10–11

Devotional Thought

God Teaches You
Study and Obey God's Word

Ezra had committed himself to study and obey the Law of the LORD. He also wanted to teach the LORD's rules and laws in Israel.

EZRA 7:10

OXO

Ezra didn't just read the Bible. He worked hard to understand what God said. He wanted to do what God said. Ezra studied what God said. Then he explained it to others. That is how God used Ezra to help many people.

Be like Ezra. Don't just read the Bible. Don't just listen to the stories. Try hard to understand what God teaches. You could try hard by listening to Bible tapes or watching Bible story videos. You could go to church and really listen to your teachers and minister. You could ask questions. And you could pray that God would help you understand. Then ask God to help do what he wants. When you do, God will use you too!

God's Angels

Don't forget to welcome strangers. By doing that, some people have welcomed angels without knowing it.

HEBREWS 13:2

O X O

All the angels were standing around the throne. They were standing around the elders and the four living creatures. They fell down on their faces in front of the throne and worshiped God. They said, *"Amen!*
May praise and glory
and wisdom be given to our God for
ever and ever.
Give him thanks and honor and
power and strength.
Amen!"

REVELATION 7:11–12

O X O

The Lord himself will come down from heaven. We will hear a loud command. We will hear the voice of the leader of the angels. We will hear a blast from God's trumpet. Many who believe in Christ will have died already. They will rise first. After that, we who are still alive and who are left will be caught up together with them. We will be taken up into the clouds. We will meet the Lord in the air. And we will be with him forever.

1 THESSALONIANS 4:16–17

God's Angels

I, Jesus, have sent my angel to give you this witness for the churches. I am the Root and the Son of David. I am the bright Morning Star.

REVELATION 22:16

All angels are spirits who serve. God sends them to serve those who will receive salvation.

HEBREWS 1:14

God is fair. He will pay back trouble to those who give you trouble. He will help you who are troubled. And he will also help us. All of those things will happen when the Lord Jesus appears from heaven. He will come in a blazing fire. He will come with the angels who are given the power to do what God wants.

2 THESSALONIANS 1:6–7

The LORD will command his angels
*   to take good care of you.*
They will lift you up in their hands.
*   Then you won't trip over a stone.*

PSALM 91:11–12

God's Words of Life on

God's Angels

I looked and heard the voice of millions and millions of angels. They surrounded the throne. They surrounded the living creatures and elders. In a loud voice they sang,
"The Lamb who was put to death, is worthy!
He is worthy to receive power and
wealth and wisdom and strength!
He is worthy to receive honor and glory and praise!"

REVELATION 5:11–12

OXO

An angel of the Lord appeared to [the shepherds]. And the glory of the Lord shone around them. They were terrified. But the angel said to them, "Do not be afraid. I bring you good news of great joy. It is for all the people. Today in the town of David a Savior has been born to you. He is Christ the Lord. Here is how you will know I am telling you the truth. You will find a baby wrapped in strips of cloth and lying in a manger." Suddenly a large group of angels from heaven also appeared. They were praising God. They said,
"May glory be given to God in the highest heaven!
And may peace be given to those he is pleased
with on earth!"

LUKE 2:9–14

God's Angels
What are Angels?

All angels are spirits who serve.

HEBREWS 1:14

OXO

What do angels look like? Some people say they have wings. Some people say they are brighter than the sun. You may not know exactly what angels look like, but you can know what they are. The Bible says that the angels are spirits who serve you!

That's right. If you love Jesus, you have your very own guardian angel. He watches over you. He talks to God about you. And he keeps you safe.

A really neat story about guardian angels can be found in the Bible book of 2 Kings. It is the story of a servant of God named Elisha. Second Kings 6:17 says, *"Elisha prayed, 'LORD, open my servant's eyes so he can see.' Then the LORD opened his eyes. He looked up and saw the hills. He saw that Elisha was surrounded by horses and chariots. Fire was all around them."*

Elisha's servant was afraid because an army was going to attack them. But Elisha knew that angels were protecting them so he asked God to show his servant the angel army ... and God did!

Next time you're afraid, open your eyes to what you can't see. Remember the power of God's love. Remember that his angels protect you. Remember that God himself has everything under control. Thank God for your guardian angel today!

Beautiful Creation

God saw everything he had made. And it was very good. ... So the heavens and the earth and everything in them were completed.

GENESIS 1:31–2:1

OXO

You placed the earth on its foundations, O God.
> *It can never be moved.*
You covered it with the oceans like a blanket.
> *The waters covered the mountains.*
But you commanded the waters, and they ran away.
> *At the sound of your thunder they rushed off.*
They flowed down the mountains.
> *They went into the valleys.*
> *They went to the place you appointed for them. ...*
You make springs pour water into the valleys.
> *It flows between the mountains.*
The springs give water to all of the wild animals.
> *The wild donkeys satisfy their thirst.*
The birds of the air build nests by the waters.
> *They sing among the branches.*
You water the mountains from your palace high in the clouds.
> *The earth is filled with the things you have made.*

PSALM 104:5–8, 10–13

Beautiful Creation

You are the one and only LORD. You made the
heavens. You made even the highest heavens.
You created all of the stars in the sky. You created
the earth and everything that is on it. And you
made the oceans and everything that is in them.
You give life to everything. Every living being in
heaven worships you.

NEHEMIAH 9:6

O X O

*The earth belongs to the LORD. And so does
        everything in it.
    The world belongs to him. And so do all
        those who live in it.
He set it firmly on the oceans.
    He made it secure on the waters.*

PSALM 24:1–2

O X O

*"Every animal in the forest already belongs to me.
    And so do the cattle on a thousand hills.
I own every bird in the mountains.
    The creatures of the field belong to me,"
        says the Lord.*

PSALM 50:10–11

Beautiful Creation

You take care of the land and water it, Lord
> *You make it very rich.*
You fill your streams with water.
> *You provide the people with grain.*
> *That's how you prepare the land.*
You water its rows.
> *You smooth out its bumps.*
You soften it with showers.
> *And you bless its crops.*
You bring the year to a close with huge crops.
> *You provide more than enough food.*
The grass grows thick even in the desert.
> *The hills are dressed with gladness.*
The meadows are covered with flocks and herds.
> *The valleys are dressed with grain.*
They sing and shout with joy.

PSALM 65:9–13

O X O

The heavens were made when the LORD
> *commanded it to happen.*
> *All of the stars were created by the breath*
> *of his mouth.*

PSALM 33:6

God's Words of Life on

Beautiful Creation

People all over the world and beyond the farthest
oceans put their hope in you, Lord.
You formed the mountains by your power.
You showed how strong you are.
You calmed the oceans and their roaring waves. ...
Those who live far away are amazed at the
miracles you have done.
What you do makes people from one end of the
earth to the other sing for joy.

PSALM 65:5–8

O X O

God is the Lord of the whole earth.
The heavens announce that what he does is right.
All people everywhere see his glory.

PSALM 97:5–6

O X O

God decides how many stars there should be.
He gives each one of them a name.

PSALM 147:4

Beautiful Creation

LORD, our Lord,
>   how majestic is your name in the whole earth!
You have made your glory
>   higher than the heavens.
You have made sure that children
>   and infants praise you. ...
I think about the heavens.
>   I think about what your fingers have created.
I think about the moon and stars
>   that you have set in place.
What is a human being that you think about him?
>   What is a son of man that you take care of
>   him?
You made him a little lower than the heavenly
>   beings.
>   You placed on him a crown of glory and
>   honor.
You made human beings the rulers over all that
>   your hands have created.
>   You put everything under their control.
They rule over all flocks and herds
>   and over the wild animals.
They rule over the birds of the air and over the fish
>   in the ocean.
>   They rule over everything that swims in the
>   oceans.
LORD, our Lord,
>   how majestic is your name in the whole
>   earth!

PSALM 8

Beautiful Creation
One Big Classroom

[King Solomon] taught about animals and birds. He also taught about reptiles and fish.

1 KINGS 4:33

OXO

Do you love flowers? Do bugs delight you? Do wriggly worms capture your attention? Do birds make your heart sing? Then you're in good company. King Solomon talked about these things. People came from around the world to learn from Solomon's wisdom about God's creation.

Do you want to be wise? First, God says you must know how great he is (Psalm 111:10). Look at the heavens (Psalm 19:1). Look at the earth (Psalm 33:5). Try to count the stars. You'll see that God has no limits. Look at a flower. You'll know that God loves beautiful things. Look closely at a bug. You'll know that God understands details. Watch a squirrel burying nuts. You'll see how God cares.

Sing with the stars. Love the flowers. Wonder at the whales. What a delightful way to learn about God!

God's Care for You

Turn all your worries over to God. He cares about you.

1 PETER 5:7

O X O

I lie down and sleep.
I wake up again, because the LORD takes care
of me.

PSALM 3:5

O X O

LORD, you bless those who do what is right.
Like a shield, your loving care keeps them
safe.

PSALM 5:12

O X O

God, you see trouble and sadness.
You take note of it. You do something about it.
So those who are attacked place themselves in
your care.

PSALM 10:14

O X O

Take good care of me, just as you would take care
of your own eyes, Lord.
Hide me in the shadow of your wings.

PSALM 17:8

God's Words of Life

God's Care for You

*From the time I was born, you took good care of me.
Ever since I came out of my mother's body,
you have been my God.*

PSALM 22:10

O X O

*The LORD takes good care of those who do what is
right.*

PSALM 37:17

O X O

*If the LORD is pleased with the way a man lives,
he makes his steps secure.
Even if the man trips, he won't fall.
The LORD's hand takes good care of him.*

PSALM 37:23–24

O X O

*You will take good care of me because I've been
honest, Lord.
You will let me be with you forever.*

PSALM 41:12

O X O

*Because you have helped me,
I sing in the shadow of your wings, Lord.
I hold on to you.
Your powerful right hand takes good care
of me.*

PSALM 63:7–8

God's Care for You

Blessed is the one who cares about weak people.
*When he is in trouble, the L*ORD* saves him.*
*The L*ORD* will guard him and keep him alive.*
He will bless him in the land.
He won't hand him over to the wishes of his
enemies.
*The L*ORD* will take care of him when he is lying sick*
in bed.
He will make him well again.

PSALM 41:1–3

He is our God.
We are the sheep belonging to his flock.
We are the people he takes good care of.

PSALM 95:7

God takes care of his flock like a shepherd.
He gathers the lambs in his arms.
He carries them close to his heart.
He gently leads those that have little ones.

ISAIAH 40:11

God's Care for You

Doesn't Anybody Care?

You are the God who sees me.

GENESIS 16:13

O X O

Are there times when nobody seems to be on your side? Even your best friend turns against you. But you are not alone. God is on your side. He sees and cares.

God has a special place in his heart for you. God stays on your side even when everyone else turns away. He notices what people do to you. He cares when you hurt. God sees when people pick on you.

Take a minute and think about all the ways God cares for you every day. Do you have clothes? Do you have a warm place to sleep at night? Do you have food? Do you even have people who love you? Wow! When you think about it, God cares for you in lots of really special ways, every single day!

Before you say, "Nobody cares!" remember that God cares. God sees you and knows what you are going through. Talk to him when you feel alone.

God's Special Gifts to You

Every good and perfect gift is from God. It comes down from the Father. He created the heavenly lights.

JAMES 1:17

O X O

The free gift of God's grace makes all of us right with him. Christ Jesus paid the price to set us free.

ROMANS 3:24

O X O

People should be satisfied with all of their hard work. That is God's gift to them.

ECCLESIASTES 3:13

O X O

We all have gifts. They differ in keeping with the grace that God has given each of us.

ROMANS 12:6

O X O

God's gift of grace was more than enough for the whole world.

ROMANS 5:15

O X O

God gives you the gift of eternal life because of what Christ Jesus our Lord has done.

ROMANS 6:23

God's Special Gifts to You

You each have your own gift from God. One has this gift. Another has that.

1 CORINTHIANS 7:7

OXO

God has given you grace that is better than anything. Let us give thanks to God for his gift. It is so great that no one can tell how wonderful it really is!

2 CORINTHIANS 9:14–15

OXO

Each one of us has received a gift of grace, just as Christ wanted us to have it. ... He is the One who gave some the gift to be apostles. He gave some the gift to be prophets. He gave some the gift of preaching the good news. And he gave some the gift to be pastors and teachers. He did it so that they might prepare God's people to serve. If they do, the body of Christ will be built up. That will continue until we all become one in the faith and in the knowledge of God's Son. Then we will be grown up in the faith. We will receive everything that Christ has for us.

EPHESIANS 4:7, 11–13

God's Special Gifts to You

You must turn away from your sins and be baptized in the name of Jesus Christ. Then your sins will be forgiven. You will receive the gift of the Holy Spirit.

ACTS 2:38

Give praise to the God and Father of our Lord Jesus Christ. In his great mercy he has given us a new birth and a hope that is alive. It is alive because Jesus Christ rose from the dead. He has given us new birth so that we might share in what belongs to him. It is a gift that can never be destroyed. It can never spoil or even fade away. It is kept in heaven for you.

1 PETER 1:3-4

Sometimes God gives a man wealth and possessions. He makes it possible for him to enjoy them. He helps him accept the life he has given him. He helps him to be happy in his work. All of those things are gifts from God.

ECCLESIASTES 5:19

God's Special Gifts to You

Unwrap Your Gift

There are different kinds of gifts. But they are all given by the same Spirit.

1 CORINTHIANS 12:4

OXO

Do you know how you can "unwrap" the special gifts God has given you? Well, first, what kinds of things do you really like to do? Are you good in sports? Do you like music? Are you friendly and cheerful? Do you love people? Do you like to speak? Do you listen well? Are you a great leader? Do you like to follow?

God is like an artist. And each person is like a work of art. He gives each of us special talents. God wants you to use your talents. He wants *you* to do something special. There are lots of things you could do with your talents, but the best thing is to use them to help others and to praise God.

Everybody is good at something. Everybody has special talents that are gifts from God. Ask God what he wants you to do with your special gifts. He will show you how you can use your talents for him while having a lot of fun too!

God's Words of Life on

Growing Up

"I will pour water out on the thirsty land.
I will make streams flow on the dry ground.
I will pour out my Spirit on your children.
I will pour out my blessing on their children after them.
They will spring up like grass in a meadow.
They will grow like poplar trees near flowing streams," says the Lord.

ISAIAH 44:3–4

Like babies that were just born, you should long for the pure milk of God's word. It will help you grow up as believers. You can do it now that you have tasted how good the Lord is.

1 PETER 2:2–3

Those who do what is right will grow like a palm tree.
They will grow strong like a cedar tree in Lebanon.
Their roots will be firm in the house of the LORD.
They will grow strong and healthy in the courtyards of our God.

PSALM 92:12–13

Growing Up

We will no longer be babies in the faith. We won't be like ships tossed around by the waves. We won't be blown here and there by every new teaching. We won't be blown around by the cleverness and tricks of people who try to hide their evil plans. Instead, we will speak the truth in love. We will grow up into Christ in every way. He is the Head. He makes the whole body grow and build itself up in love.

EPHESIANS 4:14–16

O X O

It is God who makes things grow. He is the One who is important.

1 CORINTHIANS 3:7

O X O

We pray that you will lead a life that is worthy of the Lord. We pray that you will please him in every way. So we want you to bear fruit in every good thing you do. We want you to grow to know God better.

COLOSSIANS 1:10

O X O

Have your roots in Jesus. Build yourselves up in him. Grow strong in what you believe, just as you were taught.

COLOSSIANS 2:7

God's Words of Life on

Growing Up

Grow in the grace of our Lord and Savior Jesus Christ. Get to know him better.

2 PETER 3:18

O X O

Brothers and sisters, ... be like babies as far as evil is concerned. But be grown up in your thinking.

1 CORINTHIANS 14:20

O X O

Don't let anyone look down on you because you are young. Set an example for the believers in what you say and in how you live. Also set an example in how you love and in what you believe. Show the believers how to be pure.

1 TIMOTHY 4:12

O X O

How can a young person keep his life pure?
By living in keeping with your word, Lord.
I trust in you with all my heart.
Don't let me wander away from your commands.

PSALM 119:9–10

Growing Up
Big Plans

God's got plans for you! Big plans! Beautiful plans! Maybe you will be a minister who tells people about God. Or maybe you will be a mother or father who raises children who love Jesus. Maybe you will be a famous writer or actor or leader. Or maybe you will build houses or roads or machines.

God doesn't want you to just grow from a kid to an adult. He also wants you to grow from a baby Christian to a grown-up Christian. Just like eating good food helps you grow physically, eating good spiritual food will help you grow up as a Christian.

When you were a very small baby, you drank only milk. When you grew teeth, you began to eat crackers and baby food. And now you can eat pretty much anything!

That is the same way it is with growing Christians. When you're a baby Christian you are just starting to learn about Jesus and the Bible. You drink "spiritual milk." As you become more grown up as a Christian and learn more about Jesus you start practicing obeying him. You are eating more solid spiritual food then.

So, as you grow up into an adult physically, eat good food and learn lots of new things. And, as you grow up into a strong Christian, eat good spiritual food by learning all about Jesus and obeying him in all you do.

God will help you grow up big and strong, both as a person and as a Christian!

Happiness and Joy

LORD, everything you have given me is good.
  You have made my life secure.
I am very pleased with what you have given me.
  I am very happy with what I've received
    from you.

OXO   PSALM 16:5–6

The LORD gives me strength. He is like a shield that
    keeps me safe.
  My heart trusts in him, and he helps me.
My heart jumps for joy.
  I will sing and give thanks to him.

OXO   PSALM 28:7

Our hearts are full of joy because of God.
  We trust in him, because he is holy.
LORD, may your faithful love rest on us.
  We put our hope in you.

PSALM 33:21–22

Happiness and Joy

*May those who do what is right be glad
and filled with joy when they are with God.
May they be happy and joyful.*

PSALM 68:3

O X O

God gives wisdom, knowledge and happiness to a man who pleases him.

ECCLESIASTES 2:26

O X O

*God's favor lasts for a person's whole life.
Sobbing can remain through the night.
But joy comes in the morning.*

PSALM 30:5

O X O

*You always show me the path that leads to life,
Lord.
You will fill me with joy when I am with you.
You will give me endless pleasures at your
right hand.*

PSALM 16:11

O X O

Are any of you happy? Then sing songs of praise.

JAMES 5:13

Happiness and Joy

*I will be glad and full of joy because you love me,
Lord.*

PSALM 31:7

Jesus said, "If you obey my commands, you will
remain in my love. In the same way, I have obeyed
my Father's commands and remain in his love. I
have told you this so that my joy will be in you. I
also want your joy to be complete."

JOHN 15:10–11

*Let the heavens be filled with joy. Let the earth
    be glad.
    Let them say among the nations,
      "The LORD rules!"
Let the ocean and everything in it roar.
    Let the fields and everything in them
      be glad.
Then the trees in the forest will sing with joy.
    They will sing to the LORD.*

1 CHRONICLES 16:31–33

*I trust in your faithful love, O God.
    My heart is filled with joy because you will
      save me.*

PSALM 13:5

Happiness and Joy

Let all those who go to you for safety be glad, Lord.
Let them always sing with joy.
Spread your cover over them and keep them safe.
Then those who love you will be glad because
of you.

PSALM 5:11

O X O

We are full of joy in God because of our Lord Jesus Christ. Because of him, God has brought us back to himself.

ROMANS 5:11

O X O

Jesus said, "Until now you have not asked for anything in my name. Ask, and you will receive what you ask for. Then your joy will be complete."

JOHN 16:24

O X O

Our mouths were filled with laughter.
Our tongues sang with joy.
Then the people of other nations said,
*"The L*ORD* has done great things for them."*
*The L*ORD* has done great things for us.*
And we are filled with joy.

PSALM 126:2–3

God's Words of Life on

Happiness and Joy

I will honor the LORD.

Let those who are hurting hear and be joyful.
Join me in giving glory to the LORD.

Let us honor him together.
I looked to the LORD, and he answered me.

He saved me from everything I was afraid of.
Those who look to him beam with joy.

They are never put to shame

PSALM 34:2–5

O X O

Through faith in Jesus we have received God's
grace. In that grace we stand. We are full of joy
because we expect to share in God's glory.

ROMANS 5:2

O X O

A happy heart makes a face look cheerful.

PROVERBS 15:13

O X O

May the God who gives hope fill you with great joy.
May you have perfect peace as you trust in him.
May the power of the Holy Spirit fill you with hope.

ROMANS 15:13

Happiness and Joy
God Wants You to Be Happy

The joy of the LORD makes you strong.

NEHEMIAH 8:10

OXO

What a neat story we read in Nehemiah Chapter 8. The Israelites had been crying and carrying on after they heard God's law. They felt bad because they had not lived the way God wanted them to live. Nehemiah stepped in and told them to lighten up. "Go home and enjoy special foods and sweet drinks," he said. "Don't be sad. Be joyful and enjoy."

What great advice for anyone! Forget your failures. Dry your tears. God forgives you! The joy of the Lord makes you strong.

Relax. Lift your face to the sun. Smile with God. Open your heart to his joy. Besides that, let yourself enjoy. Enjoy good foods. Enjoy pleasant days. Enjoy happy parties. Enjoy laughter and good times. God loves you and wants you to enjoy the good gifts he gives you.

Thank God today for one special thing that you enjoy. And be happy knowing that it is his present to you!

Hard Times

Blessed is the man who keeps on going when times are hard. After he has come through them, he will receive a crown. The crown is life itself. God has promised it to those who love him.

JAMES 1:12

Put up with hard times. God uses them to train you. He is treating you as children. What children are not trained by their parents? God trains all of his children.

HEBREWS 12:7–8

We are full of joy even when we suffer. We know that our suffering gives us the strength to go on. The strength to go on produces character. Character produces hope.

ROMANS 5:3–4

Who can separate us from Christ's love? Can trouble or hard times or harm or hunger? ... No! In all these things we will do even more than win! We owe it all to Christ, who has loved us.

ROMANS 8:35, 37

Hard Times

Jesus comforts us in all our troubles. Now we can comfort others when they are in trouble. We ourselves have received comfort from God. We share the sufferings of Christ. We also share his comfort.

2 CORINTHIANS 1:4–5

O X O

We think that people who don't give up are blessed. You have heard that Job was patient. And you have seen what the Lord finally did for him. The Lord is full of tender mercy and loving concern.

JAMES 5:11

O X O

God, you see trouble and sadness.
You take note of it. You do something about it.

PSALM 10:14

O X O

Suppose you suffer for being a Christian. Then don't be ashamed. Instead, praise God because you are known by that name.

1 PETER 4:16

O X O

God answered me when I was in trouble. He's been with me everywhere I've gone.

GENESIS 35:3

Hard Times

LORD, I will give you honor.
> You brought me out of deep trouble.

PSALM 30:1

O X O

God always gives you all the grace you need. So you will only have to suffer for a little while. Then God himself will build you up again. He will make you strong and steady. And he has chosen you to share in his eternal glory because you belong to Christ.

1 PETER 5:10

O X O

Suppose you suffer for doing good, and you put up with it. God will praise you for that.

1 PETER 2:20

O X O

When I was in trouble, I called out to the LORD.
> I cried to my God for help.
From his temple he heard my voice.
> My cry for help reached his ears.

PSALM 18:6

O X O

The LORD saves those who do what is right.
> He is their place of safety when trouble comes.

PSALM 37:39

Hard Times

Worth More Than Gold

Your troubles have come in order to prove that your faith is real. It is worth more than gold.

1 PETER 1:7

OXO

Gold is a precious metal. Gold is beautiful. People rushed across America to find gold. Gold would make them rich! But do you know something? There is something worth more than gold. And you may have it! Faith in Jesus is worth more than gold! Gold can't get you to heaven. But faith in Jesus can!

Sometimes gold has dirt hidden in it. Fire can melt the gold. When gold is melted any dirt bubbles to the top. Then the dirt is removed. That makes the gold pure. The purer the gold, the more it is worth. Going through fire makes gold better.

Troubles in your life are like fires that make gold pure. Bad things bubble to the top when troubles come into your life. Then God can get rid of them. Troubles make your faith pure. And the purer your faith is, the more glory and praise God will get, and the closer you will be to him! That's worth lots more than gold!

Having Faith in God

Jesus said, "If you have faith as small as a mustard seed, it is enough. You can say to this mountain, 'Move from here to there.' And it will move. Nothing will be impossible for you."

MATTHEW 17:20–21

O X O

Jesus said, "What I'm about to tell you is true. Anyone who has faith in me will do what I have been doing. In fact, he will do even greater things. That is because I am going to the Father. And I will do anything you ask in my name. Then the Son will bring glory to the Father."

JOHN 14:12–13

O X O

Let us come near to God with an honest and true heart. Let us come near with a faith that is sure and strong. Our hearts have been sprinkled. Our minds have been cleansed from a sense of guilt. Our bodies have been washed with pure water. Let us hold firmly to the hope we claim to have. The One who promised is faithful.

HEBREWS 10:22–23

Having Faith in God

Let us keep looking to Jesus. He is the author of faith. He also makes it perfect. He paid no attention to the shame of the cross. He suffered there because of the joy he was looking forward to. Then he sat down at the right hand of the throne of God.

HEBREWS 12:2

O X O

God's grace has saved you because of your faith in Christ. Your salvation doesn't come from anything you do. It is God's gift.

EPHESIANS 2:8

O X O

We are made right with God by putting our faith in Jesus Christ. That happens to all who believe.

ROMANS 3:22

O X O

Faith is being sure of what we hope for. It is being certain of what we do not see.

HEBREWS 11:1

O X O

Through Jesus and through faith in him we can approach God. We can come to him freely. We can come without fear.

EPHESIANS 3:12

Having Faith in God

The good news shows how God makes people right with himself. From beginning to end, becoming right with God depends on a person's faith. It is written, "Those who are right with God will live by faith."

ROMANS 1:17

O X O

Through faith you are kept safe by God's power.

1 PETER 1:5

O X O

We believe in the God who raised Jesus our Lord from the dead. So God will accept our faith and make us right with himself.

ROMANS 4:24

O X O

Even though you have not seen Jesus, you love him. Though you do not see him now, you believe in him. You are filled with a glorious joy that can't be put into words. You are receiving the salvation of your souls. It is the result of your faith.

1 PETER 1:8–9

O X O

Everyone who is a child of God has won the battle over the world. Our faith has won the battle for us.

1 JOHN 5:4

Having Faith in God
Check Your Roots

Have your roots in God. Build yourselves up in him. Grow strong in what you believe as you were taught.

COLOSSIANS 2:7

oxo

The roots of a tree grow under the ground. You don't see the roots. But the roots are what make a tree strong. If a tree has deep roots, it won't blow over in a storm. The roots feed the tree so it can grow up healthy. Good roots help a tree grow good fruit too.

Did you know you are like a tree? Your roots are the things you do to make your faith grow strong. Your roots are the things you do to get to know Jesus better. When you pray and read the Bible, you are growing deep roots of faith. Knowing God's words will feed your roots of faith. Your faith will become healthy and strong. And your attitude and actions will show that you are growing the way God wants you to grow. So dig deep into the Bible. Let your roots of faith grow deep in God.

Healing

*"The light of my blessing will shine on you like the
rising sun.*
I will heal you quickly.
I will march out ahead of you.
*And my glory will follow behind you and
guard you.*
*That is because I always do what is right," says the
Lord.*

ISAIAH 58:8

O X O

"I will make you healthy again.
I will heal your wounds,"
announces the LORD.

JEREMIAH 30:17

O X O

"Here is what will happen for you who have respect
for me. The sun that brings life will rise. Its rays will
bring healing to my people," says the Lord.

MALACHI 4:2

O X O

Are any of you sick? Then send for the elders of the
church to pray over you. Ask them to anoint you
with oil in the name of the Lord. The prayer offered
by those who have faith will make you well. The
Lord will heal you.

JAMES 5:14–15

Healing

God heals those who have broken hearts.
    He takes care of their wounds.

PSALM 147:3

O X O

Let's recognize him as the LORD.
    Let's keep trying to really know him.
You can be sure the sun will rise.
    And you can be just as sure the LORD will
        appear.
He will come to renew us like the winter rains.
    He will be like the spring rains that water
        the earth."

HOSEA 6:3

O X O

Jesus went into the villages, the towns and the countryside. Everywhere he went, the people brought the sick to the market places. Those who were sick begged him to let them touch just the edge of his clothes. And all who touched him were healed.

MARK 6:56

O X O

I will praise the LORD.
    I won't forget anything he does for me.
He forgives all my sins.
    He heals all my sicknesses.

PSALM 103:2–3

Healing

LORD my God, I called out to you for help.
And you healed me.

PSALM 30:2

O X O

Here is something else I remember.
And it gives me hope.
The LORD loves us very much.
So we haven't been completely destroyed.
His loving concern never fails.
His great love is new every morning.
LORD, how faithful you are!
I say to myself, "The LORD is everything I will ever
need.
So I will put my hope in him."
The LORD is good to those who put their hope in
him.
He is good to those who look to him.
It is good when people wait quietly
for the LORD to save them.

LAMENTATIONS 3:21–26

O X O

A man's cheerful heart gives him strength when he
is sick.

PROVERBS 18:14

Healing
Inside and Out

Jesus said, "Is it easier to say to this [crippled] man, 'Your sins are forgiven'? Or to say, 'Get up, take your mat and walk'?"

MARK 2:9

OXO

Have you ever been really sick or hurt? Maybe you couldn't even walk. Your family had to carry you or you had to ride in a wheelchair. Did you feel like no one understood how bad you felt? Jesus knows how you feel. He cares about how you feel. Maybe you aren't sick or hurt on the outside, but you hurt on the inside, in your heart. You might be lonely or afraid. Maybe you feel ashamed. Jesus knows about how you feel inside too.

What does Jesus care about most? Your insides or your outsides? He cares about both! In the story of the crippled man in Mark 2:1–12, Jesus forgave the man's sins, then he healed him, inside and out. He cared about the man's hurt legs. But the man's broken heart was just as important as his legs. Jesus is powerful. And he cares about you, inside and out! You can take all of your hurts to him.

Heaven

We know that God raised the Lord Jesus from the dead. And he will also raise us up with Jesus. He will bring ... you to God in heaven.

2 CORINTHIANS 4:14

O X O

We are citizens of heaven. And we can hardly wait for a Savior from there. He is the Lord Jesus Christ. He has the power to bring everything under his control. By his power he will change our earthly bodies. They will become like his glorious body.

PHILIPPIANS 3:20–21

O X O

The Lord himself will come down from heaven. We will hear a loud command. We will hear the voice of the leader of the angels. We will hear a blast from God's trumpet. Many who believe in Christ will have died already. They will rise first. After that, we who are still alive and are left will be caught up together with them. We will be taken up in the clouds. We will meet the Lord in the air. And we will be with him forever.

1 THESSALONIANS 4:16–17

O X O

Jesus said, "Blessed are you when people make fun of you and hurt you because of me. You are also blessed when they tell all kinds of evil lies about you because of me. Be joyful and glad. Your reward in heaven is great."

MATTHEW 5:11–12

Heaven

The Spirit took me to a huge, high mountain. He showed me Jerusalem, the Holy City. It was coming down out of heaven from God. It shone with the glory of God. It gleamed like a very valuable jewel. ... The foundations of the city walls were decorated with every kind of jewel. ... The 12 gates were made from 12 pearls. Each gate was made out of a single pearl. The main street of the city was made out of pure gold, as clear as glass. I didn't see a temple in the city. This was because the Lamb and the Lord God who rules over all are its temple. The city does not need the sun or moon to shine on it. God's glory is its light, and the Lamb is its lamp. ... Its gates will never be shut, because there will be no night there. ... Then the angel showed me the river of the water of life. It was as clear as crystal. It flowed from the throne of God and of the Lamb.

REVELATION 21:10–11, 19, 21–23, 25; 22:1

From heaven the LORD looks down
	and sees everyone.
From his throne he watches
	all those who live on the earth.
He creates the hearts of all people.

PSALM 33:13–15

God's Words of Life on

Heaven

I saw the Holy City, the new Jerusalem. It was coming down out of heaven from God. It was prepared like a bride beautifully dressed for her husband. I heard a loud voice from the throne. It said, "Now God makes his home with people. He will live with them. They will be his people. And God himself will be with them and be their God. He will wipe away every tear from their eyes. There will be no more death or sadness. There will be no more crying or pain. Things are no longer the way they used to be." He who was sitting on the throne said, "I am making everything new!" Then he said, "Write this down. You can trust these words. They are true." He said to me, "It is done. I am the Alpha and the Omega, the First and the Last. I am the Beginning and the End. Anyone who is thirsty may drink from the spring of the water of life. It doesn't cost anything! Anyone who overcomes will receive all this from me. I will be his God, and he will be my child."

REVELATION 21:2–7

We know that the earthly tent we live in will be destroyed. But we have a building made by God. It is a house in heaven that lasts forever.

2 CORINTHIANS 5:1

God's first and only Son is over all things. God's people share in what belongs to his Son. Their names are written in heaven.

HEBREWS 12:23

Heaven

How to Know You Will Live Forever

God has given us eternal life. That life is found in his Son.

1 JOHN 5:11

OXO

God doesn't want you to worry that you may not make it to heaven. God wants everyone to live forever with him. That is why God sent his only Son, Jesus. That's why God gave you the Bible. God wants you to have eternal life. He wants you to live forever in heaven. And God wants you to know that you will. For sure!

God promised eternal life to everyone who believes in Jesus. Have you asked Jesus to forgive your sins? If you have, you can know God heard that prayer. You can know because you are asking for something that God wants to give you! And you can know you have eternal life in heaven. For sure!

In heaven there will be no dark nights. God's love will make everything bright. Everyone will live in peace. No one will fight. No one will get sick. No one will die. No one will cry. Everyone will love each other and love God.

What a wonderful way to live! Imagine that! Someday you will see it. God has promised that someday you will live there. What a wonderful promise!

Jesus

God sent the angel Gabriel to Nazareth, a town in Galilee. He was sent to a virgin. ... The virgin's name was Mary. ... The angel said to her, "Do not be afraid, Mary. God is very pleased with you. You will become pregnant and give birth to a son. You must name him Jesus. He will be great and will be called the Son of the Most High God. The Lord God will make him a king like his father David of long ago. He will rule forever over his people, who came from Jacob's family. His kingdom will never end."

LUKE 1:26–27, 30–33

O X O

Joseph went from the town of Nazareth in Galilee to Judea. That is where Bethlehem, the town of David, was. Joseph went there because he belonged to the family line of David. He went there with Mary to be listed. Mary was engaged to him. She was expecting a baby. While Joseph and Mary were there, the time came for the child to be born. She gave birth to her first baby. It was a boy. She wrapped him in large strips of cloth. Then she placed him in a manger. There was no room for them in the inn.

LUKE 2:4–7

God's Words of Life on

Jesus

Jesus went all over Galilee. There he taught in the synagogues. He preached the good news of God's kingdom. He healed every illness and sickness the people had.

MATTHEW 4:23

O X O

The governor's soldiers took Jesus into the palace. ... They took off his clothes and put a purple robe on him. Then they twisted thorns together to make a crown. They placed it on his head. They put a stick in his right hand. Then they fell on their knees in front of him and made fun of him. "We honor you, king of the Jews!" they said. They spit on him. They hit him on the head with the stick again and again.

MATTHEW 27:27–30

O X O

The soldiers brought them to the place called The Skull. There they nailed Jesus to the cross. He hung between the two criminals. One was on his right and one was on his left. Jesus said, "Father, forgive them. They don't know what they are doing." ... It was now about noon. The whole land was covered with darkness until three o'clock. The sun had stopped shining. The temple curtain was torn in two. Jesus called out in a loud voice, "Father, into your hands I commit my very life." After he said this, he took his last breath.

LUKE 23:33–34, 44–46

Jesus

The Sabbath day was now over. It was dawn on the first day of the week. Mary Magdalene and the other Mary went to look at the tomb [where Jesus was buried]. There was a powerful earthquake. An angel of the Lord came down from heaven. The angel went to the tomb. ... The angel said to the women, "Don't be afraid. I know that you are looking for Jesus, who was crucified. He is not here! He has risen, just as he said he would! Come and see the place where he was lying. Go quickly! Tell his disciples, 'He has risen from the dead.' " ... So the women hurried away from the tomb. They were afraid, but they were filled with joy. They ran to tell the disciples. Suddenly Jesus met them. "Greetings!" he said. They came to him, took hold of his feet and worshiped him.

MATTHEW 28:1–2, 5–9

O X O

Jesus said, "All authority in heaven and on earth has been given to me. So you must go and make disciples of all nations. Baptize them in the name of the Father and of the Son and of the Holy Spirit. Teach them to obey everything I have commanded you. And you can be sure that I am always with you, to the very end."

MATTHEW 28:18–20

Devotional Thought on

Jesus

Jesus is the Word

In the beginning, the Word was already there.
The Word was with God, and the Word was God.
He was with God in the beginning. All things were
made through him.

JOHN 1:1-3

OXO

Who's the Word? Who became a human
being? Who lived on earth?

Jesus! He is God. His human name is Jesus.
His God name is Christ, or Word. Change "the
Word" to "Jesus" when you read the verse above.
You can see how great Jesus is.

All things were created through Jesus. He
made the sun, moon, and stars. He made the
earth. He made everything in the earth. He
created you!

Everything was created for Jesus. The sun,
moon and stars are his. Everything in it is his.
You are his!

Jesus holds everything together. The world
lives because Jesus lives. The world stays together
because Jesus lives. You live because Jesus lives!

Some of this is a mystery, isn't it? But all of it
is a comfort. Imagine how great Jesus is. Think
about how much he loves you!

Laughing

God has given laughter to me.

GENESIS 21:6

O X O

There is a time to cry.
And there's a time to laugh.
There is a time to be sad.
And there's a time to dance.

ECCLESIASTES 3:4

O X O

Jesus said, "Blessed are you who are sad now.
You will laugh."

LUKE 6:21

O X O

Our mouths were filled with laughter.
Our tongues sang with joy.
Then the people of other nations said,
"The LORD has done great things for them."
The LORD has done great things for us.
And we are filled with joy.

PSALM 126:2–3

O X O

God will fill your mouth with laughter.
Shouts of joy will come from your lips.

JOB 8:21

Laughing
Surprise!

Sarah said, "God has given laughter to me. Everyone who hears about this will laugh with me."

GENESIS 21:6

OXO

Does God laugh? Does he surprise you sometimes? Yes!

Sarah could not have a baby because she was too old. Her husband Abraham was even older. He was 100! But God surprised them. He gave them Isaac, their first son. Sarah was so happy. No wonder she laughed!

Has God ever surprised you? Maybe he answered a prayer, or sent you a new friend. Maybe he made the sun come out on a rainy day so that you could play outside.

Pay attention. Watch for God's surprises. Sometimes they will make you laugh out loud!

Listening to God

*I will listen to what God the L*ord *will say.*
He promises peace to his faithful people.

PSALM 85:8

O X O

He is our God.
We are the sheep belonging to his flock.
We are the people he takes good care of.
Listen to his voice today.

PSALM 95:7

O X O

Let wise people listen and add to what they have
learned.
Let those who understand what is right get
guidance.

PROVERBS 1:5

O X O

*The L*ord *and King has taught me what to say.*
He has taught me how to help those who
are tired.
He wakes me up every morning.
He makes me want to listen like a good
student.
*The L*ord *and King has unplugged my ears.*
I've always obeyed him.
I haven't turned away from him.

ISAIAH 50:4–5

God's Words of Life on

Listening to God

"Listen and come to me.
Pay attention to me.
Then you will live.
I will make a covenant with you that will last forever.
I will give you my faithful love," says the Lord.

ISAIAH 55:3

Jesus said, "Some people come to me and listen to me and do what I say. I will show you what they are like. They are like someone who builds a house. He digs down deep and sets it on solid rock. When a flood comes, the river rushes against the house. But the water can't shake it. The house is well built."

LUKE 6:47–48

Jesus said, "My sheep listen to my voice. I know them, and they follow me. I give them eternal life, and they will never die. No one can steal them out of my hand. My Father, who has given them to me, is greater than anyone. No one can steal them out of my Father's hand."

JOHN 10:27–29

Those whose hearts understand what is right get
knowledge.
The ears of those who are wise listen for it.

PROVERBS 18:15

131

Listening to God

My dear brothers and sisters, pay attention to what I say. Everyone should be quick to listen. But they should be slow to speak.

JAMES 1:19

Jesus came to a village where a woman named Martha lived. She welcomed him into her home. She had a sister named Mary. Mary sat at the Lord's feet listening to what he said. But Martha was busy with all the things that had to be done. She came to Jesus and said, "Lord, my sister has left me to do the work by myself. Don't you care? Tell her to help me!" "Martha, Martha," the Lord answered. "You are worried and upset about many things. But only one thing is needed. Mary has chosen what is better. And it will not be taken away from her."

LUKE 10:38–42

Jesus said, "Everyone who listens to the Father and learns from him comes to me."

JOHN 6:45

Jesus answered, "I came into the world to give witness to the truth. Everyone who is on the side of truth listens to me."

JOHN 18:37

Listening to God
Are You Paying Attention?

We must pay more careful attention to what we have heard. Then we will not drift away from it.

HEBREWS 2:1

OXO

Suppose your mom asked you to do something. But you were watching TV. You listened a little. But you weren't really paying attention. You may have said, "Uh-huh." Then you forgot what she said. It drifted from your mind. So you forgot to do what she asked.

The same thing can happen with God's Word. If you don't pay attention, you will forget what it says. Then you won't do what it says.

Pay attention to God's Word. Listen carefully. Think about what you hear. Ask a grown-up questions about it. Make sure you understand enough so you can do what God says. Then you won't drift away from what you hear. And it won't drift away from you.

Loving God

To love God with all your heart and mind and strength is very important.

MARK 12:33

O X O

Let all those who look to you
be joyful and glad because of what you
have done, LORD.
Let those who love you because you save them
always say,
"May the LORD be honored!"

PSALM 40:16

O X O

Those who love you will be glad because of you,
Lord.

PSALM 5:11

O X O

I love you, LORD.
You give me strength.

PSALM 18:1

O X O

LORD, I love the house where you live.
I love the place where your glory is.

PSALM 26:8

Loving God

Love the Lord, all of you who are faithful to him!
The Lord watches over the faithful.

PSALM 31:23

O X O

Those who love God are known by God.

1 CORINTHIANS 8:3

O X O

I love the Lord, because he heard my voice.
He heard my cry for his favor.
Because he paid attention to me,
I will call out to him as long as I live.

PSALM 116:1–2

O X O

Lord, I really love your law!
All day long I spend time thinking about it.

PSALM 119:97

O X O

Here is what it means to love God. It means that
we obey his commands. And his commands are not
hard to obey.

1 JOHN 5:3

Loving God

I love your commands more than gold.
I love them more than pure gold.
I consider all of your rules to be right, Lord.

PSALM 119:127–128

OXO

The LORD watches over all those who love him.

PSALM 145:20

OXO

Turn to me and show me your favor, O Lord.
That's what you've always done for those
who love you.

PSALM 119:132

OXO

Those who love your law enjoy great peace, O God.
Nothing can make them trip and fall.

PSALM 119:165

OXO

I will sing a song for the LORD.
He is the one I love.

ISAIAH 5:1

Loving God

No eye has seen,
no ear has heard,
no mind has known
what God has prepared for those who love
him.

1 CORINTHIANS 2:9

O X O

We know that in all things God works for the good of those who love him.

ROMANS 8:28

O X O

May grace be given to everyone who loves our Lord Jesus Christ with a love that will never die.

EPHESIANS 6:24

O X O

I want you to realize that the LORD your God is God. He is the faithful God. He keeps his covenant for all time to come. He keeps it with those who love him and obey his commands. He shows them his love.

DEUTERONOMY 7:9

O X O

Jesus said, "'Love the Lord your God with all your heart and with all your soul. Love him with all your mind.' This is the first and most important commandment."

MATTHEW 22:37–38

God's Words of Life on

Loving God

Jesus said, "Anyone who has my commands and obeys them loves me. My Father will love the one who loves me. I too will love him. And I will show myself to him. ... Anyone who loves me will obey my teaching. My Father will love him. We will come to him and make our home with him."

JOHN 14:21, 23

O X O

Blessed is the man who keeps on going when times are hard. After he has come through them, he will receive a crown. The crown is life itself. God has promised it to those who love him.

JAMES 1:12

O X O

Even though you have not seen Jesus, you love him. Though you do not see him now, you believe in him. You are filled with a glorious joy that can't be put into words.

1 PETER 1:8

O X O

Your promises have proved to be true, O Lord. I love them.

PSALM 119:140

Loving God
Man Overboard!

"It is the Lord!" As soon as Peter heard that, he put his coat on. He had taken it off earlier. Then he jumped into the water.

JOHN 21:7

OXO

All the disciples loved Jesus. But only one went overboard!

After Jesus died and rose again, the disciples went fishing. Jesus called to them from the shore. Peter couldn't wait to see Jesus! He jumped out the boat, into the water and headed for Jesus! Maybe his friends laughed. But Peter didn't care. His love for Jesus was all that mattered. He couldn't wait for the boat to get to shore. His love made him leap! His love made him *do* something!

Do you love Jesus like this? Are you happy that Jesus is alive? Jesus wants your love for him to make you happy. What do you do that shows your love? Go overboard in your love for Jesus. And do something to show it!

Loving Others

Dear friends, let us love one another, because love comes from God. Everyone who loves has been born again because of what God has done. That person knows God.

1 JOHN 4:7

O X O

Love must be honest and true. ... Love each other deeply. Honor others more than yourselves.

ROMANS 12:9–10

O X O

Love is patient. Love is kind. It does not want what belongs to others. It does not brag. It is not proud. It is not rude. It does not look out for its own inter-ests. It does not easily become angry. It does not keep track of other people's wrongs. Love is not happy with evil. But it is full of joy when the truth is spoken. It always protects. It always trusts. It always hopes. It never gives up. Love never fails.

1 CORINTHIANS 13:4–8

O X O

Those who love their brothers and sisters are living in the light.

1 JOHN 2:10

Loving Others

Dear children, don't just talk about love. Put your love into action. Then it will truly be love. That's how we know that we hold to the truth.

1 JOHN 3:18–19

O X O

Serve one another in love. The whole law can be found in a single command. "Love your neighbor as you love yourself."

GALATIANS 5:13–14

O X O

The three most important things to have are faith, hope and love. But the greatest of them is love.

1 CORINTHIANS 13:13

O X O

The only thing that really counts is faith that shows itself through love.

GALATIANS 5:6

O X O

Be completely gentle. Be patient. Put up with one another in love. The Holy Spirit makes you one in every way. So try your best to remain as one. Let peace keep you together.

EPHESIANS 4:2–3

God's Words of Life on

Loving Others

You are the children that God dearly loves. So be just like him. Lead a life of love, just as Christ did. He loved us. He gave himself up for us.

EPHESIANS 5:1–2

O X O

I pray that your love will grow more and more. And let it be based on knowledge and understanding. Then you will be able to know what is best. You will be pure and without blame until the day Christ returns. You will be filled with the fruit of right living produced by Jesus Christ. All of those things bring glory and praise to God.

PHILIPPIANS 1:9–11

O X O

You are God's chosen people. You are holy and dearly loved. So put on tender mercy and kindness as if they were your clothes. Don't be proud. Be gentle and patient. Put up with each other. Forgive the things you are holding against one another. Forgive, just as the Lord forgave you. And over all of those good things put on love. Love holds them all together perfectly as if they were one.

COLOSSIANS 3:12–14

Loving Others
Born to Love

Anyone who does not love does not know God, because God is love.

1 JOHN 4:8

OXO

Do you know someone who goes to church, but doesn't love others? They may know their memory verse. They may dress nicely. They may sit quietly during church. They may say they love Jesus. But something is wrong if they don't love people.

This verse says, "God is love." God shows his love by loving you and loving others. He wants you to share his love by loving others, too. Loving God and loving people go together. You can tell if someone loves God. You will see love in their life.

Everyone needs God's help to love. When you accept Jesus as Savior, you become a child of God. Everyone born into God's family is born to love. So, don't just say you love God. Show it by loving people too. Let God's love grow in you. Love is what you were born for!

Money

Money that is gained in the wrong way disappears. But money that is gathered little by little grows.

PROVERBS 13:11

O X O

Jesus sat down across from the place where people put their temple offerings. He watched the crowd putting their money into the offering boxes. Many rich people threw large amounts into them. But a poor widow came and put in two very small copper coins. They were worth much less than a penny. Jesus asked his disciples to come to him. He said, "What I'm about to tell you is true. That poor widow has put more into the offering box than all the others. They all gave a lot because they are rich. But she gave even though she is poor. She put in everything she had. She gave all she had to live on."

MARK 12:41–44

O X O

Don't be controlled by love for money. Be happy with what you have. God has said,
"I will never leave you.
I will never desert you."
So we can say boldly,
"The Lord helps me. I will not be afraid.
What can a mere man do to me?"

HEBREWS 13:5–6

Money

The godly are always giving and lending freely.
    Their children will be blessed.

PSALM 37:26

O X O

Jesus said, "When you give to the needy, don't let your left hand know what your right hand is doing. Then your giving will be done secretly. Your Father will reward you. He sees what you do secretly."

MATTHEW 6:3–4

O X O

Honor the LORD with your wealth.
    Give him the first share of all your crops.
    Then your storerooms will be so full they
        can't hold everything.

PROVERBS 3:9–10

O X O

Some give freely but get even richer.
    Others don't give what they should but get
        even poorer.
Anyone who gives a lot will succeed.
    Anyone who renews others will be renewed.

PROVERBS 11:24–25

O X O

Godly people give without holding back.

PROVERBS 21:26

Money

Those who give to poor people
will have everything they need.

PROVERBS 28:27

O X O

Give, and it will be given to you. A good amount
will be poured into your lap. It will be pressed
down, shaken together, and running over. The same
amount you give will be measured out to you.

LUKE 6:38

O X O

Jesus said, "Little flock, do not be afraid. Your Father
has been pleased to give you the kingdom. Sell
what you own. Give to those who are poor. Provide
purses for yourselves that will not wear out. Put
away riches in heaven that will not be used up.
There, no thief can come near it. There, no moth can
destroy it. Your heart will be where your riches are."

LUKE 12:32–34

O X O

Jesus said, "Don't worry. Don't say, 'What will we
eat?' Or, 'What will we drink?' Or, 'What will we
wear?' People who are ungodly run after all of those
things. Your Father who is in heaven knows that you
need them. But put God's kingdom first. Do what
he wants you to do. Then all of those things will
also be given to you."

MATTHEW 6:31–33

Devotional Thought on

Money

Something to Give

A poor widow came and put in two very small copper coins. They were worth much less than a penny.

MARK 12:42

OXO

Giving is for everyone! It's not just for grown-ups. It's not just for rich people. Anyone can give. You can give too!

You can give part of your allowance to church. You can give time to help your mom around the house. You can give your old toys to children who need them.

The widow in the Bible story gave a lot—even though what she gave was worth less than a penny. She gave what she had to God. And Jesus blessed her for it.

What can you give today? You may not have much. But you *always* have something to give!

Obeying

Those who obey what they are taught
guard their lives.

PROVERBS 19:16

The LORD's love
for those who have respect for him
lasts for ever and ever.
Their children's children will know
that he always does what is right.
He always loves those who keep his covenant.
He always does what is right for those who
remember to obey his commands.

PSALM 103:17–18

I will lead a full and happy life,
because I've tried to obey your rules, Lord.

PSALM 119:45

Children, obey your parents as believers in the Lord.
Obey them because it's the right thing to do.
Scripture says, "Honor your father and mother." That
is the first commandment that has a promise.
"Then things will go well with you. You will live a
long time on the earth."

EPHESIANS 6:1–3

Obeying

Jesus said, "Just as the Father has loved me, I have loved you. Now remain in my love. If you obey my commands, you will remain in my love. In the same way, I have obeyed my Father's commands and remain in his love. I have told you this so that my joy will be in you. I also want your joy to be complete. Here is my command. Love each other, just as I have loved you. No one has greater love than the one who gives his life for his friends. You are my friends if you do what I command."

JOHN 15:9–14

O X O

*The law that brings respect for the L*ORD *is pure.*
*   It lasts forever.*
*The directions the L*ORD *gives are true.*
*   All of them are completely right.*
They are more priceless than gold.
*   They have greater value than huge amounts*
*   of pure gold.*
They are sweeter than honey
*   that is taken from the honeycomb.*
I am warned by them.
*   When I obey them, I am greatly rewarded.*

PSALM 19:9–11

149

Obeying

Jesus said, "Blessed are those who hear God's word and obey it."

LUKE 11:28

O X O

Jesus saves all those who obey him.

HEBREWS 5:9

O X O

You have been chosen in keeping with what God the Father had planned. That happened through the Spirit's work to make you pure and holy. God chose you so that you might obey Jesus Christ. He wanted you to be made clean by the blood of Christ. May more and more grace and peace be given to you.

1 PETER 1:2

O X O

God has commanded us to believe in the name of his Son, Jesus Christ. He has also commanded us to love one another. Those who obey his commands remain joined to him. And he remains joined to them.

1 JOHN 3:23–24

O X O

The way we show our love is to obey God's commands. He commands you to lead a life of love.

2 JOHN 1:6

Obeying
Control Yourself

We must control ourselves. We must do what is right. We must lead godly lives in today's world.

TITUS 2:12

O X O

Don't talk in class. Don't chew gum. Don't pass notes. Rules, rules, rules. They are not much fun, are they? But God wants you to obey the rules. Why?

Rules help you to get along with each other better. What if everyone talked in class? You wouldn't learn anything. And you would get a headache from all the noise!

Rules also help you to train yourself. When you obey rules, you are training yourself to act a certain way. You prove that you can take care of yourself. And that proves you are growing up!

Suppose your parents went away and told you, "Don't mess up the house! Find something good to do while we're away. If you obey us, we will bring you a surprise." Would you mess up the house? Of course not! You'd find something good to do, wouldn't you?

The Bible says that Jesus went away to heaven. He promised to return. And while he's gone, he doesn't want you to mess up. He wants you to say no to doing wrong things. He wants you to find something good to do. So, obey Jesus while he is away. If you do, he has promised you a good reward when he returns.

151

Patience

I was patient while I waited for the L<small>ORD</small>.
He turned to me and heard my cry for help.
He brought me up out of the mud and dirt.
He set my feet on a rock.
He gave me a firm place to stand on.

PSALM 40:1–2

Anyone who is patient has great understanding.

PROVERBS 14:29

A man who burns with anger stirs up fights.
But a person who is patient calms things
down.

PROVERBS 15:18

It's better to be patient than proud.

ECCLESIASTES 7:8

We want you to be very strong, in keeping with
God's glorious power. We want you to be patient.
Never give up. Be joyful as you give thanks to the
Father. He has made you fit to share with all his
people. You will all receive a share in the kingdom
of light.

COLOSSIANS 1:11–12

Patience

It is better to be patient than to fight.

PROVERBS 16:32

O X O

We hope for what we don't have yet. So we are patient as we wait for it.

ROMANS 8:25

O X O

Love is patient.

1 CORINTHIANS 13:4

O X O

The fruit the Holy Spirit produces is love, joy and peace. It is being patient, kind and good. It is being faithful and gentle and having control of oneself.

GALATIANS 5:22–23

O X O

A man's wisdom makes him patient.
He will be honored if he forgives someone
who sins against him.

PROVERBS 19:11

Patience

Be like those who have faith and are patient. They will receive what God promised.

HEBREWS 6:12

OXO

Brothers and sisters, be patient until the Lord comes. See how the farmer waits for the land to produce its rich crop. See how patient he is for the fall and spring rains. You too must be patient. You must stand firm. The Lord will soon come back.

JAMES 5:7–8

OXO

God's people need to be very patient. They are the ones who obey God's commands. They remain faithful to Jesus.

REVELATION 14:12

OXO

Let us not become tired of doing good. At the right time we will gather a crop if we don't give up.

GALATIANS 6:9

OXO

A huge cloud of witnesses is all around us. So let us throw off everything that stands in our way. Let us throw off any sin that holds on to us so tightly. Let us keep on running the race marked out for us. Let us keep looking to Jesus. He is the author of faith. He also makes it perfect.

HEBREWS 12:1–2

Devotional Thought on

Patience

It Takes Patience

You too must be patient.

OXO

If you plant a daisy seed, will a daisy quickly pop up from the ground? No! A daisy takes a long time to grow.

First, the seed grows beneath the soil. Then a tiny plant appears. It takes weeks to grow. Then a flower bud forms. That too must grow. Finally, it will open.

Lots of small wonders happen under the ground and inside the plant. You can't see them all. You will finally see a daisy. But you must wait calmly. You must be patient.

You must wait calmly for God, too. If you ask him something, you may think that he will never answer. But he will, at the right time.

You can't watch an answer grow. God makes changes that you can't see. He works in people's hearts. He makes small wonders happen.

God will answer at the right time. You will see his answer. You will feel his love.

God will answer. Wait calmly and patiently. Remember your daisy.

Praising God

*I will give thanks to the LORD because he does
what is right.
I will sing praise to the LORD Most High.*

PSALM 7:17

Give praise to the One who is able to keep you from
falling into sin. He will bring you into his heavenly
glory without any fault. He will bring you there with
great joy. Give praise to the only God. He is our
Savior. Glory, majesty, power and authority belong to
him. Give praise to him through Jesus Christ our
Lord. Give praise to the One who was before all time,
who now is, and who will be forever. Amen.

JUDE 1:24–25

*The LORD gave me a new song to sing.
It is a hymn of praise to our God.
Many people will see what he has done and will
worship him.
They will put their trust in the LORD.*

PSALM 40:3

Give praise to the God and Father of our Lord Jesus
Christ! He is the Father who gives tender love. All
comfort comes from him.

2 CORINTHIANS 1:3

Praising God

I will praise the LORD. He gives me good advice.
Even at night my heart teaches me.
I know that the LORD is always with me.
He is at my right hand.
I will always be secure.

PSALM 16:7–8

O X O

People will praise God because you obey him. That proves that you really believe the good news about Christ. They will also praise God because you share freely with them and with everyone else.

2 CORINTHIANS 9:13

O X O

All day long we talk about how great God is.
We will praise your name forever, Lord.

PSALM 44:8

O X O

Give praise to the God and Father of our Lord Jesus Christ. In his great mercy he has given us a new birth and a hope that is alive. It is alive because Jesus Christ rose from the dead.

1 PETER 1:3

157

Praising God

Because of what you have done, Lord,
I will praise you in the whole community of
those who worship you.
In front of those who respect you,
I will keep my promises.
Those who are poor will eat and be satisfied.
Those who look to the LORD will praise him.
May their hearts be filled with new hope!

PSALM 22:25–26

OXO

Give praise to the God and Father of our Lord Jesus
Christ. He has blessed us with every spiritual bless-
ing. Those blessings come from the heavenly world.
They belong to us because we belong to Christ.

EPHESIANS 1:3

OXO

Lord, I will praise you among the nations.
I will sing about you among the people of
the earth.
Great is your love. It reaches to the heavens.
Your truth reaches to the skies.
God, may you be honored above the heavens.
Let your glory be over the whole earth.

PSALM 57:9–11

Praising God

I will thank the LORD at all times.
My lips will always praise him.
I will honor the LORD.
Let those who are hurting hear and be joyful.
Join me in giving glory to the LORD.
Let us honor him together.
I looked to the LORD, and he answered me.
He saved me from everything I was afraid of.
Those who look to him beam with joy.
They are never put to shame.

PSALM 34:1–5

Let us never stop offering to God our praise through Jesus. Let us offer it as the fruit of lips that say they believe in him.

HEBREWS 13:15

God, your fame reaches from one end of the earth
to the other.
In the same way, people praise you from
one end of the earth to the other.
You use your power to do what is right.

PSALM 48:10

159

Praising God

Lord, I will praise you with all my heart.
I will tell about all of the miracles you have
done.
I will be glad and full of joy because of you.
Most High God, I will sing praise to you.

PSALM 9:1–2

O X O

Are any of you happy? Then sing songs of praise.

JAMES 5:13

O X O

I will praise you forever for what you have done,
Lord.
I will put my hope in you because you are
good.
I will praise you when I'm with your faithful people.

PSALM 52:9

O X O

Jesus said, "Let your light shine in front of others.
Then they will see the good things you do. And they
will praise your Father who is in heaven."

MATTHEW 5:16

Praising God
Keep On Praising!

Saul's daughter Michal was watching from a window. She saw King David leaping and dancing in the sight of the LORD. That made her hate him in her heart.

2 SAMUEL 6:16

O X O

David loved God more than anything. Loving God made David so happy that he had to dance! When David danced for God, David's wife felt ashamed. She told David to stop dancing. But he said, "No!" David was filled with joy. And he would not let anyone take his joy away.

God wants you to love him more than anything. He wants you to find joy! Have you ever had fun praising God? God wants you to be happy when you praise him. Maybe you will be so happy you will get up and jump for joy! Don't let anybody stop you from loving God and showing it. Maybe they will see how happy you are and they will praise God with you!

Prayer

"You will call out to me. You will come and pray to me. And I will listen to you. When you look for me with all your heart, you will find me," says the Lord.

JEREMIAH 29:12–13

Let's lift up our hands to God in heaven.
Let's pray to him with all our hearts.

LAMENTATIONS 3:41

Jesus said, "When you pray, go into your room. Close the door and pray to your Father, who can't be seen. He will reward you. Your Father sees what is done secretly."

MATTHEW 6:6

The Holy Spirit helps us when we are weak. We don't know what we should pray for. But the Spirit himself prays for us. He prays with groans too deep for words. God, who looks into our hearts, knows the mind of the Spirit. And the Spirit prays for God's people just as God wants him to pray.

ROMANS 8:26–27

God's Words of Life on

Prayer

Don't worry about anything. Instead, tell God about everything. Ask and pray. Give thanks to him. Then God's peace will watch over your hearts and your minds because you belong to Christ Jesus. God's peace can never be completely understood.

PHILIPPIANS 4:6–7

O X O

The LORD our God is near us every time we pray to him.

DEUTERONOMY 4:7

O X O

Let everyone who is godly pray to you, Lord
while they can still look to you.
When troubles come like a flood,
they certainly won't reach those who are
godly.

PSALMS 32:6

O X O

At all times, pray by the power of the Spirit. Pray all kinds of prayers. Be watchful, so that you can pray. Always keep on praying for all of God's people.

EPHESIANS 6:18

Prayer

Jesus said, "This is how you should pray.

"'Our Father in heaven,
may your name be honored.
May your kingdom come.
May what you want to happen be done
on earth as it is done in heaven.
Give us today our daily bread.
Forgive us our sins,
just as we also have forgiven those who sin
against us.
Keep us from falling into sin when we are tempted.
Save us from the evil one.'"

MATTHEW 6:9–13

"My house will be called
a house where people from all nations can
pray," says the Lord.

ISAIAH 56:7

Pray for everyone. Ask God to bless them. Give thanks for them. Pray for kings. Pray for all who are in authority. Pray that we will live peaceful and quiet lives. And pray that we will be godly and holy. That is good. It pleases God our Savior. He wants everyone to be saved. He wants them to come to know the truth.

1 TIMOTHY 2:1–4

Prayer

Dear friends, build yourselves up in your most holy faith. Let the Holy Spirit guide and help you when you pray.

JUDE 1:20

O X O

The LORD has heard my cry for his favor.
The LORD accepts my prayer.

PSALM 6:9

O X O

There is one thing we can be sure of when we come to God in prayer. If we ask anything in keeping with what he wants, he hears us. If we know that God hears what we ask for, we know that we have it.

1 JOHN 5:14–15

O X O

The Lord's eyes look with favor on those who are godly.
His ears are open to their prayers.

1 PETER 3:12

O X O

Let us boldly approach the throne of grace. Then we will receive mercy. We will find grace to help us when we need it.

HEBREWS 4:16

God's Words of Life on

Prayer

Are any of you in trouble? Then you should pray. Are any of you happy? Then sing songs of praise. Are any of you sick? Then send for the elders of the church to pray over you. Ask them to anoint you with oil in the name of the Lord. The prayer offered by those who have faith will make you well. The Lord will heal you. If you have sinned, you will be forgiven. So admit to one another that you have sinned. Pray for one another so that you might be healed.

JAMES 5:13–16

OXO

During the day the LORD sends his love to me.
During the night I sing about him.
I say a prayer to the God who gives me life.

PSALM 42:8

OXO

Jesus said, "If you believe, you will receive what you ask for when you pray."

MATTHEW 21:22

OXO

The LORD is ready to help all those who call out to
him.
He helps those who really mean it when
they call out to him.
He satisfies the needs of those who have respect
for him.
He hears their cry and saves them.

PSALM 145:18–19

Prayer
When It's Too Good to Be True

"Peter is at the door!" she exclaimed. "You're out of your mind," they said to her. But she kept telling them it was true.

ACTS 12:14–15

OXO

Peter had been arrested. The believers met together to pray. They asked God to free Peter from prison.

God heard their prayers. He sent an angel to free Peter from his chains. When Peter got out of prison, he went straight to the prayer meeting.

A young girl named Rhoda heard Peter's voice. But this seemed too good to be true! She was so excited she didn't even let him in! She ran away to tell the people that were praying that God had answered their prayers. They didn't believe her! They thought she was crazy! But Peter knocked so loudly that they finally let him in.

God hears your prayers too. And nothing is too hard for God. Do you expect God to answer? When you pray, get ready for your answer to come. It may almost seem too good to be true. But God will answer!

God's Words of Life on

Rest

Jesus said, "Come to me, all of you who are tired and are carrying heavy loads. I will give you rest. Become my servants and learn from me. I am gentle and free of pride. You will find rest for your souls. Serving me is easy, and my load is light."

MATTHEW 11:28–30

OXO

God gives strength to those who are tired.
He gives power to those who are weak.
Even young people become worn out and get tired.
Even the best of them trip and fall.
But those who trust in the LORD
will receive new strength.
They will fly as high as eagles.
They will run and not get tired.
They will walk and not grow weak.

ISAIAH 40:29–31

OXO

Let the one the LORD loves rest safely in him.
The LORD guards him all day long.
The one the LORD loves rests in his arms.

DEUTERONOMY 33:12

OXO

The person who rests in the shadow of the Most High God
will be kept safe by the Mighty One.

PSALM 91:1

Rest

The LORD lets me lie down in fields of green grass.
He leads me beside quiet waters.
He gives me new strength.
He guides me in the right paths
for the honor of his name.

PSALM 23:2–3

O X O

Doing what is right will bring peace and rest.
When my people do that, they will stay calm
and trust in the LORD forever.
They will live in a peaceful land.
Their homes will be secure.
They will enjoy peace and quiet.

ISAIAH 32:17–18

O X O

"Stand where the roads cross, and look around.
Ask where the old paths are.
Ask for the good path, and walk on it.
Then your hearts will find rest in me," says
the Lord.

JEREMIAH 6:16

Rest

God lives forever! You can run to him for safety.
His powerful arms are always there to
carry you.

DEUTERONOMY 33:27

"I will give rest to those who are tired. I will satisfy those who are weak," says the Lord.

JEREMIAH 31:25

I lie down and sleep.
I wake up again, because the LORD takes
care of me.

PSALM 3:5

The LORD and King is the Holy One of Israel. He says,
"You will find peace and rest
when you turn away from your sins and
depend on me.
You will receive the strength you need
when you stay calm and trust in me."

ISAIAH 30:15

I will find my rest in God alone.
He is the One who gives me hope.

PSALM 62:5

Rest

Get Some Rest!

Jesus said to his apostles, "Come with me by yourselves to a quiet place. You need to get some rest."

MARK 6:31

O X O

Think of the last time you were really, really tired. I bet you were crabby. You dragged your body around like an old sack. All you thought about was bed!

Jesus knows that you get tired. And that's okay. When you're tired, he doesn't yell at you. He doesn't make you do more or work harder. Instead he says, "You need to be with me in a quiet place. You need to get some rest."

Next time you're tired, go with Jesus to a quiet place. Lie on your back in the grass. Sit under a tree. Or let Jesus tuck you into bed! He loves to be with you, even when you're tired or sleeping.

Sharing the Good News

Jesus said, "You must go and make disciples of all nations. Baptize them in the name of the Father and of the Son and of the Holy Spirit. Teach them to obey everything I have commanded you. And you can be sure that I am always with you, to the very end."

MATTHEW 28:19–20

God promised the good news long ago. He announced it through his prophets in the Holy Scriptures. The good news is about God's Son. As a human being, the Son of God belonged to King David's family line. By the power of the Holy Spirit, he was appointed to be the mighty Son of God because he rose from the dead. He is Jesus Christ our Lord.

ROMANS 1:2–4

I am not ashamed of the good news. It is God's power. And it will save everyone who believes.

ROMANS 1:16

Sharing the Good News

You must keep your faith steady and firm. Don't move away from the hope that the good news holds out to you. It is the good news that you heard. It has been preached to every creature under heaven.

COLOSSIANS 1:23

You ... became believers in Christ. That happened when you heard the message of truth. It was the good news about how you could be saved. When you believed, he marked you with a seal. The seal is the Holy Spirit that he promised.

EPHESIANS 1:13

Treasure is kept in clay jars. In the same way, we have the treasure of the good news in these earthly bodies of ours. That shows that the mighty power of the good news comes from God. It doesn't come from us.

2 CORINTHIANS 4:7

O X O

All over the world the good news is bearing fruit and growing.

COLOSSIANS 1:6

Sharing the Good News

Pray that the Lord's message will spread quickly. Pray that others will honor it just as you did.

2 THESSALONIANS 3:1

O X O

Make sure in your hearts that Christ is Lord. Always be ready to give an answer to anyone who asks you about the hope you have. Be ready to give the reason for it. But do it gently and with respect.

1 PETER 3:15

O X O

Don't forget to do good. Don't forget to share with others. God is pleased with those kinds of offerings.

HEBREWS 13:16

O X O

God loved the world so much that he gave his one and only Son. Anyone who believes in him will not die but will have eternal life.

JOHN 3:16

O X O

Faith comes from hearing the message. And the message that is heard is the word of Christ.

ROMANS 10:17

Sharing the Good News

I Could Go On and On ...

Lord, I will praise you among the nations.
I will sing about you among the people of
the earth.

PSALM 57:9

OXO

Have you ever had a new puppy or kitten or even a great new toy? Did you love it so much you felt happy every time you saw it? Did you want to tell everyone about it? When you feel love, it makes you happy. When you are happy, you want to share how you feel. You want to talk about the one you love.

God loves you. He wants you to love him too. When you and God love each other, you will be happy. Then you will want to share how you feel. You will want to talk about God. You will want to share how you feel about God with others. Tell everybody about God so they can love him too. Who can you tell about God today?

175

Telling the Truth

Jesus said, "I am the way and the truth and the life. No one comes to the Father except through me."

JOHN 14:6

O X O

I know that you want truth to be in my heart, Lord. You teach me wisdom deep down inside me.

PSALM 51:6

O X O

Don't let love and truth ever leave you.
Tie them around your neck.
Write them on the tablet of your heart.
Then you will find favor and a good name
in the eyes of God and people.

PROVERBS 3:3–4

O X O

The Most High God is like a shield that keeps me safe.
He saves those whose hearts are honest.

PSALM 7:10

O X O

God is pleased with people who tell the truth.

PROVERBS 12:22

Telling the Truth

Kings are pleased when what you say is honest.
They value people who speak the truth.

PROVERBS 16:13

O X O

A person must do what is right.
He must be honest and tell the truth. ...
A person like that will be kept safe.
It will be as if he were living on high
mountains.
It will be as if he were living in a mountain fort.
He will have all of the food he needs.
And he will never run out of water.

ISAIAH 33:15–16

O X O

God will make your godly ways shine like the dawn.
He will make your honest life shine like the
sun at noon.

PSALM 37:6

O X O

Truthful words last forever.
But lies last for only a moment.

PROVERBS 12:19

Telling the Truth

Buy the truth. Don't sell it.
Get wisdom, training and understanding.

PROVERBS 23:23

O X O

Anyone who lives by the truth comes into the light.

JOHN 3:21

O X O

The LORD loves those who are honest.
He will not desert those who are faithful to
him.
They will be kept safe forever.

PSALM 37:28

O X O

The mouths of those who do what is right speak
words of wisdom.
They say what is honest.
God's law is in their hearts.
Their feet do not slip.

PSALM 37:30–31

O X O

You will take good care of me because I've been
honest.
You will let me be with you forever, Lord.

PSALM 41:12

Telling the Truth
Be a Wise Guy!

Thoughtless words cut like a sword.
But the tongue of wise people brings healing.

PROVERBS 12:18

O X O

Do you know people who talk without thinking? They say things that aren't true. They don't think before they speak. Then their lies get them into trouble and hurt people's feelings. They probably didn't even mean to hurt anyone, but they just didn't think. Not very wise, is it?

Wise people think before they speak and they always tell the truth. They think about how their words will make someone feel. If their words might hurt someone, *they don't say them*! When their words would make someone feel happy, they make sure to say them. They practice using true, kind words. That is wise.

Practice thinking before you speak. Do your words make people feel better or do they make them feel bad? Practice saying kind things and true things to others, not things that hurt others. Then your words will make people feel good and you will have many friends. That's really being a wise guy!

Trusting God

Trust in the LORD with all your heart.
Do not depend on your own understanding.
In all your ways remember him.
Then he will make your paths smooth and
straight.

PROVERBS 3:5–6

O X O

You brought me out of my mother's body.
You made me trust in you
even when I was at my mother's breast.
From the time I was born, you took good care of me.
Ever since I came out of my mother's body,
you have been my God.

PSALM 22:9–10

O X O

Sinful people have all kinds of trouble.
But the LORD's faithful love
is all around those who trust in him.

PSALM 32:10

O X O

May the God who gives hope fill you with great joy.
May you have perfect peace as you trust in him.

ROMANS 15:13

Trusting God

I trust in your faithful love, O God.
My heart is filled with joy because you will
save me.
I will sing to the LORD.
He has been so good to me.

PSALM 13:5–6

O X O

Our people of long ago put their trust in you, Lord.
They trusted in you, and you saved them.
They cried out to you and were saved.
They trusted in you, and you didn't let them
down.

PSALM 22:4–5

O X O

Our hearts are full of joy because of him.
We trust in him, because he is holy.
LORD, may your faithful love rest on us.
We put our hope in you.

PSALM 33:21–22

O X O

Trust in the LORD and do good.
Then you will live in the land and enjoy its
food.
Find your delight in the LORD.
Then he will give you everything your heart
really wants.

PSALM 37:3–4

Trusting God

Some trust in chariots. Some trust in horses.
But we trust in the LORD our God.
They are brought to their knees and fall down.
But we get up and stand firm.

PSALM 20:7–8

O X O

I trust in you, LORD.
I say, "You are my God."
My whole life is in your hands.

PSALM 31:14–15

O X O

Trust in God at all times, you people.
Tell him all of your troubles.
God is our place of safety.

PSALM 62:8

O X O

LORD, those who know you will trust in you.
You have never deserted those who look to you.

PSALM 9:10

O X O

Jesus said, "Do not let your hearts be troubled. Trust in God. Trust in me also."

JOHN 14:1

Devotional Thought on

Trusting God
Just Trust

Do not depend on your own understanding.

PROVERBS 3:5

OXO

Imagine that you must find your way to a park on the other side of town. Do you need directions? Better yet, can an adult take you there?

You are standing near the beginning of your life. What's ahead? How long will you go to school? Whom will you marry? What work will you do?

God says that you don't need to figure everything out by yourself. You will face choices. But you won't face them alone.

Trust God completely. Remind yourself that God walks with you every day. He knows the way.

If you trust him, God says he'll help you through life. He'll guide you through the choices. What if the way twists and turns? What will happen when the going gets rough? God will pick you up and carry you through!

Ask God to stay close to you and help you to stay close to him. Every day, thank God that he leads you and that you can always trust in him!

183

God's Words of Life

For When You Feel Afraid

I trust in God. I praise his word.
    I trust in God. I will not be afraid.
    What can people do to me?

PSALM 56:4

O X O

Even though I walk
    through the darkest valley,
I will not be afraid.
    You are with me, Lord.
Your shepherd's rod and staff
    comfort me.

PSALM 23:4

O X O

The person who rests in the shadow of the Most
        High God
    will be kept safe by the Mighty One.
I will say about the Lord,
    "He is my place of safety.
He is like a fort to me.
    He is my God. I trust in him."

PSALM 91:1–2

God's Words of Life

For When You Feel Afraid

God is our place of safety. He gives us strength.
He is always there to help us in times of
trouble.
The earth may fall apart.
The mountains may fall into the middle of
the sea.
But we will not be afraid.
The waters of the sea may roar and foam.
The mountains may shake when the waters
rise.
But we will not be afraid.

PSALM 46:1–3

O X O

The LORD gives me light and saves me.
Why should I fear anyone?
The LORD is my place of safety.
Why should I be afraid?

PSALM 27:1

God's Words of Life on

For When You Feel Afraid

God will cover you with his wings.
> Under the feathers of his wings you will find
> safety.
> He is faithful. He will keep you safe like a
> shield or a tower.

PSALM 91:4

O X O

I looked to the LORD, and he answered me.
> He saved me from everything I was afraid of.

PSALM 34:4

O X O

The LORD is the one who keeps you safe.
> So let the Most High God be like a home to
> you.

PSALM 91:9

O X O

"Be strong and brave. Do not be terrified. Do not
lose hope. I am the LORD your God. I will be with
you everywhere you go," says the LORD.

JOSHUA 1:9

For When You Feel Afraid

I Trust in God!

When I'm afraid,
I will trust in you, Lord.

PSALM 56:3

OXO

Nobody likes to feel afraid. Fear is a terrible feeling! Fear can put scary thoughts in your mind! Fear is powerful! It can keep you from sleeping. It can keep you from making new friends. It can keep you from going places.

What makes you feel afraid? Do thunderstorms and lightning scare you? Maybe it's that lump in your stomach when you have to get on the school bus for the first day of school. God can help you when you feel afraid. God is stronger than anything that makes you afraid. God is with you when you turn out the lights. God is with you when you meet new friends. He's with you when you try new things. God is not afraid of anything! And he will help you when you are afraid.

Remember that you can ask God to help you anytime and anywhere!

187

Working

*Blessed are all those who have respect for the
LORD.*
    They live as he wants them to live.
Your work will give you what you need.
    Blessings and good things will come to you.

PSALM 128:1–2

O X O

Hands that don't want to work make you poor.
    But hands that work hard bring wealth to you.
A child who gathers crops in summer is wise.

PROVERBS 10:4–5

O X O

Hands that work hard will rule.

PROVERBS 12:24

O X O

*People who refuse to work want things and get
nothing.*
    *But the longings of people who work hard
are completely satisfied.*

PROVERBS 13:4

O X O

All hard work pays off.

PROVERBS 14:23

Working

The plans of people who work hard succeed.

PROVERBS 21:5

O X O

Do you see a man who does good work?
He will serve kings.
He won't serve ordinary people.

PROVERBS 22:29

O X O

People should be satisfied with all of their hard work. That is God's gift to them.

ECCLESIASTES 3:12

O X O

Work at everything you do with all your heart. Work as if you were working for the Lord, not for human masters. Work because you know that you will finally receive as a reward what the Lord wants you to have. You are serving the Lord Christ.

COLOSSIANS 3:23

O X O

I work hard with all of Christ's strength. His strength works powerfully in me.

COLOSSIANS 1:29

Working

Work as if you were not serving people but the Lord. You know that the Lord will give you a reward. He will give to each of you in keeping with the good you do.

EPHESIANS 6:7

O X O

God makes the whole body grow and build itself up in love. Under the control of Christ, each part of the body does its work. It supports the other parts. In that way, the body is joined and held together.

EPHESIANS 4:16

O X O

Do your best to please God. Be a worker who doesn't need to be ashamed.

2 TIMOTHY 2:15

O X O

Because I belong to Christ Jesus, I can take pride in my work for God.

ROMANS 15:17

Working
Rewarding Work

The Son of Man is going to come in his Father's glory. His angels will come with him. And he will reward everyone in keeping with what they have done.

MATTHEW 16:27

O X O

What is a reward? It's something you work for. And it's something you look forward to.

Your mom rewards you for cleaning your room by giving you money. Your teacher rewards you for your hard work by giving you good grades. A judge rewards you for your project by giving you a blue ribbon.

When you go to heaven, Jesus will reward you for what you have done. He will look at how you obeyed your parents and how you treated your friends. He will remember how you showed your love for him. And his reward will be better than anything money can buy. Better then good grades. And better than a thousand blue ribbons!

Jesus can't wait to reward you. Will you work hard for him?

Worry

Jesus said, "Don't worry about your life and what you will eat or drink. And don't worry about your body and what you will wear. Isn't there more to life than eating? Aren't there more important things for the body than clothes?

"Look at the birds of the air. They don't plant or gather crops. They don't put away crops in storerooms. But your Father who is in heaven feeds them. Aren't you worth much more than they are? Who can add even one hour to your life by worrying?

"And why do you worry about clothes? See how the wild flowers grow. They don't work or make clothing. But here is what I tell you. Not even Solomon in all of his glory was dressed like one of those flowers.

"If that is how God dresses the wild grass, won't he dress you even better? After all, the grass is here only today. Tomorrow it is thrown into the fire. ...

"So don't worry. Don't say, 'What will we eat?' Or, 'What will we drink?' Or, 'What will we wear?' People who are ungodly run after all of those things. Your Father who is in heaven knows that you need them. But put God's kingdom first. Do what he wants you to do. Then all of those things will also be given to you.

"So don't worry about tomorrow. Tomorrow will worry about itself."

MATTHEW 6:25–34

God's Words of Life on

Worry

Don't worry about anything. Instead, tell God about everything. Ask and pray. Give thanks to him. Then God's peace will watch over your hearts and your minds because you belong to Christ Jesus.

PHILIPPIANS 4:6–7

O X O

"I will bless any man who trusts in me.
        I will show my favor to the one who
                depends on me.
He will be like a tree that is planted near water.
        It sends out its roots beside a stream.
It is not afraid when heat comes.
        Its leaves are always green.
It does not worry when there is no rain.
        It always bears fruit," says the Lord.

JEREMIAH 17:7–8

O X O

Those who listen to [wisdom] will live in safety.
        They will not worry. They won't be afraid of
                getting hurt.

PROVERBS 1:33

O X O

Worry makes a man's heart heavy.
        But a kind word cheers him up.

PROVERBS 12:25

Worry

I said, "My foot is slipping."
But LORD, your love kept me from falling.
I was very worried.
But your comfort brought joy to my heart.

PSALM 94:18–19

My spirit, why are you so sad?
Why are you so upset deep down inside
me?
Put your hope in God.
Once again I will have reason to praise him.
He is my Savior and my God.

PSALM 42:5–6

OXO

Turn your worries over to the LORD.
He will keep you going.
He will never let godly people fall.

PSALM 55:22

OXO

Turn all your worries over to God. He cares about you.

1 PETER 5:7

God's Words of Life on

Worry

Trust in the LORD with all your heart.
Do not depend on your own understanding.
In all your ways remember him.
*Then he will make your paths smooth and
straight.*

PROVERBS 3:5–6

O X O

*Save your people. Bless those who belong to you,
Lord.*
Be their shepherd. Take care of them forever.

PSALM 28:9

O X O

Those who trust in the LORD are like Mount Zion.
*They will always be secure. They will last
forever.*

PSALM 125:1

O X O

The LORD gives strength to his people.
The LORD blesses his people with peace.

PSALM 29:11

O X O

*Give praise to the Lord. Give praise to God our
Savior.*
He carries our heavy loads day after day.

PSALM 68:19

Worry

God didn't give us a spirit that makes us weak and fearful. He gave us a spirit that gives us power and love.

2 TIMOTHY 1:7

O X O

God is our place of safety. He gives us strength.
He is always there to help us in times of
trouble.

PSALM 46:1

O X O

I will continue to carry you even when you are old.
I will take good care of you even when your
hair is gray.
I have made you. And I will carry you.
I will take care of you. And I will save you.
I am the LORD.

ISAIAH 46:4

O X O

I hold on to you, Lord.
Your powerful right hand takes good care of
me.

PSALM 63:8

Devotional Thought on

Worry

Worry, Worry

Jesus said, "I tell you, do not worry."

MATTHEW 6:25

O✗O

You can't sleep at night. You're upset. Your stomach is tied up in knots. You're nervous. You can't get your mind to rest. You're uptight. You think, think, think all the time. That's worry.

You worry about many things. Grades. Fights with friends. Tornados. Bombs. Earthquakes. Death. There is a lot to worry about!

But worrying doesn't help anything. It won't raise your grades. It won't torpedo a tornado. And it won't shake an earthquake. It's useless!

Next time you're worried, think about God first. Do what he wants you to do. Then trust him to take care of the rest, because he will!

You are God's Child

*"As a mother comforts her child,
    I will comfort you," says the Lord.*

ISAIAH 66:13

O X O

Jesus called a little child over to him. He had the child stand among them. Jesus said, "What I'm about to tell you is true. You need to change and become like little children. If you don't, you will never enter the kingdom of heaven. Anyone who becomes as free of pride as this child is the most important in the kingdom of heaven."

MATTHEW 18:2–4

O X O

You didn't receive a spirit that makes you a slave to fear once again. Instead you received the Holy Spirit, who makes you God's child. By the Spirit's power we call God "Abba." Abba means Father. The Spirit himself joins with our spirits. Together they give witness that we are God's children. As his children, we will receive all that he has for us.

ROMANS 8:15–17

O X O

Everyone who is a child of God has won the battle over the world.

1 JOHN 5:4

You are God's Child

The LORD says, "Can a mother forget the baby
who is nursing at her breast?
Can she stop showing her tender love
to the child who was born to her?
She might forget her child.
But I will not forget you.
I have written your name on the palms of my hands".

ISAIAH 49:15–16

Jesus took a little child and had the child stand among them. Then he took the child in his arms. He said to them, "Anyone who welcomes one of these little children in my name welcomes me. And anyone who welcomes me doesn't welcome only me but also the One who sent me."

MARK 9:36–37

"I will be your Father.
You will be my sons and daughters,"
says the Lord who rules over all.

2 CORINTHIANS 6:18

You are God's Child

People were bringing little children to Jesus. They wanted him to touch them. But the disciples told the people to stop. When Jesus saw this, he was angry. He said to his disciples, "Let the little children come to me. Don't keep them away. God's kingdom belongs to people like them. What I'm about to tell you is true. Anyone who will not receive God's kingdom like a little child will never enter it." Then he took the children in his arms. He put his hands on them and blessed them.

MARK 10:13–16

O X O

How great is the love the Father has given us so freely! Now we can be called children of God. And that's what we really are!

1 JOHN 3:1

O X O

The right time came. God sent his Son. A woman gave birth to him. He was born under the authority of the law. He came to set free those who were under the law. He wanted us to be adopted as children with all the rights children have. Because you are his children, God sent the Spirit of his Son into our hearts. He is the Holy Spirit. By his power we call God "Abba." Abba means Father. So you aren't slaves any longer. You are God's children. Because you are his children, he gives you what he promised to give his people.

GALATIANS 4:4–7

You are God's Child
Child of God

Dear children, you belong to God. ... The One who is in you is more powerful than the one who is in the world.

1 JOHN 4:4

O X O

What does God call you?

What if God called you his slave? Slaves work really hard. They don't get paid. And the master doesn't love them.

What if God called you his student? Students have to sit and learn. They have to do what the teacher says. And the teacher always grades their work.

But God doesn't call you his slave. He doesn't call you his student. He calls you his child! You are a child of God! That means you're related to God. You belong to him. He is your Father. He takes care of you, and he loves you, no matter what.

What a great God! What a wonderful Father!

You are God's Helper in the World

The one who plants and the one who waters have the same purpose. The Lord will give each of us a reward for our work. We work together with God. You are like God's field. You are like his building.

1 CORINTHIANS 3:8–9

OXO

God is fair. He will not forget what you have done. He will remember the love you have shown him. You showed it when you helped his people. And you show it when you keep on helping them.

HEBREWS 6:10

OXO

The Spirit of the LORD and King is on me.
The LORD has anointed me
to tell the good news to poor people.
He has sent me to comfort
those whose hearts have been broken. ...
He has sent me to announce the year
when he will set his people free.
He wants me to announce the day
when he will pay his enemies back.
Our God has sent me
to comfort all those who are sad.

ISAIAH 61:1–2

You are God's Helper in the World

Brothers and sisters, we are asking you to warn those who don't want to work. Cheer up those who are shy. Help those who are weak. Put up with everyone. Make sure that nobody pays back one wrong act with another. Always try to be kind to each other and to everyone else.

1 THESSALONIANS 5:14–15

O X O

God has appointed apostles in the church. Second, he has appointed prophets. Third, he has appointed teachers. Then he has appointed people who do miracles and those who have gifts of healing. He also appointed those able to help others, those able to direct things, and those who can speak in different kinds of languages they had not known before.

1 CORINTHIANS 12:28

O X O

Say only what will help to build others up and meet their needs. Then what you say will help those who listen.

EPHESIANS 4:29

O X O

God will give eternal life to those who keep on doing good. They want glory, honor, and life that never ends.

ROMANS 2:7

God's Words of Life

You are God's Helper in the World

Bless those who hurt you. Bless them, and do not call down curses on them. Be joyful with those who are joyful. Be sad with those who are sad. Agree with each other. Don't be proud. Be willing to be a friend of people who aren't considered important. Don't think that you are better than others.

ROMANS 12:14–16

OXO

Jesus will say, "My Father has blessed you. Come and take what is yours. It is the kingdom prepared for you since the world was created. I was hungry. And you gave me something to eat. I was thirsty. And you gave me something to drink. I was a stranger. And you invited me in. I needed clothes. And you gave them to me. I was sick. And you took care of me. I was in prison. And you came to visit me.'

Then the people who have done what is right will answer him. "Lord," they will ask, "when did we see you hungry and feed you? When did we see you thirsty and give you something to drink? When did we see you as a stranger and invite you in? When did we see you needing clothes and give them to you? When did we see you sick or in prison and go to visit you?"

[Jesus] will reply, "What I'm about to tell you is true. Anything you did for one of the least important of these brothers of mine, you did for me."

MATTHEW 25:34–40

You are God's Helper in the World

Please, Let Me!

Then I heard the voice of the Lord. He said, "Who will I send? Who will go for us?" I said, "Here I am. Send me!"

ISAIAH 6:8

OXO

When someone asks for help, do you say, "Let me! Let me!" Or do you say, "Do I have to?" Some people only do what they have to do. Some people do more than they have to do. Doing more than you have to do is special. People notice extra effort. You can surprise people by doing more than they expect.

Just doing what you have to do is okay. Doing more than you have to do is better. It may take extra work. It may take extra time. But you will be making God really happy and he will be really proud of you.

You see, God doesn't need anyone to help him. He can do anything! But, because he loves you and wants to help you learn to be like Jesus, he lets you help him by helping others.

So surprise people by doing more than they expect you to. It's fun to see the surprised look on their faces. You may have to work a little harder, but remember that you're helping God. Your hard work will really be worth it!

God's Words of Life

My Favorite Verses

OXO

_____

_____

_____

_____

_____

_____

_____

_____

_____

_____

_____

My Favorite Verses

OXO

_____

_____

_____

_____

_____

_____

_____

_____

_____

_____

_____

_____

At Inspirio we love to hear from you—your
stories, your feedback,
and your product ideas.
Please send your comments to us
by way of e-mail at
icares@zondervan.com
or to the address below:

Attn: Inspirio Cares
5300 Patterson Avenue SE
Grand Rapids, MI 49530

If you would like further information
about Inspirio and the products we
create please visit us at:
www.inspiriogifts.com

Thank you and God Bless!